Sing It Make It Say It Pray It

and

other ways
to write
God's Word
on
your heart!

 Abingdon Press

SING IT, MAKE IT, SAY IT, PRAY IT
and Other Ways to Write God's Word on Your Heart

ISBN 0-687-02770-5

To Shari Latta,
whose busy hands
make happy hearts.

02 03 04 05 06 07 08 09 10 11 – 10 9 8 7 6 5 4 3 2 1

Manufactured in the United States of America

Table of Contense

Teachers! Here is a book after your own heart...

Sing It
Make It
Say It
Pray It

And Other Ways to Write God's Word on Your Heart

Bible Verses: Fifty-seven beloved verses to help your kids cherish and remember God's word

Activities: Crafts, songs, snacks, games, prayers, stewardship, outdoor adventures, choral responses, and worship

Materials: Inexpensive, easy-to-find supplies

Ready?

Are you ready to lead fun, spirit-filled activities that will energize and inspire elementary-aged kids in your church, school, or camp?

Set

This book is set up to be teacher-friendly, offering a variety of activities with simple options and lesson-extending ideas.

Go

Goodbye to the days of boring, rote memorization. Go ahead and make Scripture meaningful and memorable with these creative lessons!

Before You Get Going

Bible Verse: "You show that you are a letter of Christ, prepared by us, written not with ink but with the Spirit of the living God, not on tablets of stone but on tablets of human hearts." (2 Corinthians 3:3)

Activity: Before your begin the activities in this book, have kids make Heart Tablets for recording the verses they learn.

Materials: Bible, this book, construction paper, white or colored paper, pencils, hole punch, scissors, cloth ribbon, puff paints

Ready

Cut hearts from 9 by 12 inch sheets of construction paper, two per child, for the front and back covers of the tablet. Cut hearts from 8 1/2 by 11 inch sheets of white or colored paper that will form the inside pages of the tablets. You will need to add more pages from time to time, but begin with five to ten sheets per child.

Punch holes in the top of the paper heart covers and pages, one on each side. Narrow cloth ribbon works best for binding the tablets together, since it can be tied and retied. Cut ribbon into 14 inch lengths, two per child.

Set

Put the paper hearts, lengths of ribbon, and pencils on the table. As kids arrive, ask them to write their names in bold or fancy letters across construction paper hearts. Then show them how to put the tablets together. The ribbon is best tied in a bow.

Go!

When this is done, hold up the Bible and **ask:** What is this? *(the Bible, God's word)* Why do we need to know God's word? *(Because it teaches us about God, Jesus, and our Christian faith and shows how God wants us to live.)*
Say: One of the ways that the Bible is different from most books, is that the Bible is divided into verses. There are many verses in the Bible that stand out as being especially meaningful. By learning and remembering these verses, we can carry God's

5

word in our hearts and minds forever. Open the Bible, and read the verse, then have the kids say it with you. Next, hold up this book.

Say: This book was written just for you! It is filled with lively and fun activities, each based around a Bible verse. As we do an activity, you will be writing it on your hearts, which means that you will understand the verse and remember it. Just a little while ago, you assembled a Heart Tablet. When a Bible verse activity is finished, you will record that verse in your tablet to help you remember. Bring out the puff paints. Tell the kids to trace over their names with the paint and decorate the rest of the cover. Set the tablets aside to dry.

Pray: When the tablets are decorated, ask kids to cross their hands over their hearts. **Pray:** Dear God, As we begin the activities in our new book, help us to write the words from your book, the Bible, forever on the tablets of our hearts. Amen.

As each activity is finished, have kids write the verse on the tablets. You may need to assist younger children. Kids may want to illustrate the verse and write a comment or two about the activity.

Another Go

Get kids ready and set to go on these Bible verse adventures by serving a heart-shaped snack and leading them in singing a heart song such as "Down in My Heart."

Bouncing Feet

PRAISE HIM WITH TAMBOURINE AND DANCE

Bible Verse: "Praise him with tambourine and dance; praise him with strings and pipe!" (Psalm 150:4)

Activity: Kids will make their own tambourines to use in dances that they choreograph.

Materials: Bible, paper plates, stapler, jingle bells, stickers, crayons or markers, crepe paper streamers, player and music

Ready:

Make a sample tambourine. You will need two paper plates for each child. With markers or crayons, on the back of both of the plates write: "PRAISE" in bright, bold letters. Then decorate the plates any way you like using the crayons or markers and stickers. Place three or four jingle bells between the two plates, with undecorated sides facing one another. Staple around the edges, attaching crepe paper streamers as you go.

You will need music for dancing. Consider Christian music that the kids know.

Set:

As the kids arrive, have the music playing. With your tambourine in hand, do a bit of dancing. Go ahead and be silly! The kids will love it.

Go!:

When all the kids have arrived, turn off the music and have the kids sit down.

Ask: What was I doing when you arrived today? (*shaking a tambourine and dancing*)

Say: I was praising God with music and dancing. Listen to a Bible verse that talks about praising God with music and dance. Open your Bible and read the verse, then have the kids say it with you.

Ask: Do any of you play a musical instrument? After the kids respond, **say:** The tambourine was one of the musical instruments used during worship in Bible times. Other instruments included the trumpet, a stringed instrument called a lyre, cymbals, and flutes.

Then ask: Do any of you take dancing lessons or like to dance? After the kids respond, **say:** In the Bible, dance is often linked with rejoicing and celebration. Sometimes dance was used as part of worship. Today, in honor of our Bible verse, we're going to praise God with tambourines and dancing.

Have the kids make their tambourines. When they are finished, **say:** And now it's time for the celebration to begin.

Ask for a volunteer who will be the first Dance Instructor. The Dance Instructor will lead the group in a dance he or she creates. (If you can't recruit a Dance Instructor, you may need to begin and hopefully the kids will then take turns at the role.) Explain that the Dance Instructor may make up any sort of serious or silly dance. The tambourines should be part of the dance. Remind boys that many of the world's great dancers and dance instructors have been men.

Start the music and after the Dance Instructor has led the group in a song, recruit more Dance Instructors.

Pray:

When the dancing is finished, ask the kids to put down their tambourines, form a circle, and join hands. Say that in Bible times, circle dances were one form of dance. Ask kids to slowly move in a circle as you **pray:** Dear God, We praised you today with tambourine and dance. Thank you for our joyful celebration. Amen.

Another Go:

Kids enjoy the hymn, "The Lord of the Dance," found in most contemporary hymnals. Set to the old Shaker tune, "Simple Gifts," the hymn was written in 1963 by British poet, folk singer, and songwriter, Sidney Carter.

FOLLOW ME

Bible Verse: "And Jesus said to them, 'Follow me and I will make you fish for people.'" (Mark 1:17)

Activity: Kids will link arms and form a Chain of Disciples as one by one they are invited to "Follow me."

Materials: Bible, blue or green yarn, ribbon, or crepe paper

Ready:

Kids will spread apart and one by one, be invited to link arms in a Chain of Disciples. Consider conducting the activity with your kids and then having them help you, on another occasion such as a church picnic or homecoming, make a Chain of Disciples with a larger group.

Set:

In the center of your space, lay the yarn in a large circle. This is the Sea of Galilee. As kids come into the room, **say:** My, the Sea of Galilee is warm today. Touch your toes in it. And I hear the fishing is good today, too.

Go:!

When everyone has arrived, gather the group together and begin. (You may sit around the Sea of Galilee, if this is practical.)

Say: When Jesus began his ministry, he needed people to help him. One day he went up to two fishermen, Simon Peter and Andrew, who were fishing in the Sea of Galilee. Listen to what happened.

Open the Bible and read Mark 1:16-20. Then read verse 17 again and have the kids say it with you.

Ask: What did Jesus mean when he said, "I will make you fish for people?" Did he mean that they were to catch people in their fishing nets? *(No, Jesus wanted them to help him with his ministry. He wanted them to tell others about Jesus.)*

Say: Two fishermen, Simon Peter and Andrew, were the first disciples. But Jesus wants us to be disciples, too.

Ask: How can we be disciples? *(tell others about God, Jesus, and our Christian faith; invite others to come to our church; show Christian love to others)*

Continue: In honor of the first disciples and to help us think about being disciples, we're going to create a Chain of Disciples.

Explain how the chain works. The first person approaches a second person saying: "Follow Me!" They link elbows and the second person leads them to a third. The first two say: "Follow Me!" Then the second person links elbows with the third. This continues until everyone is in the chain.

Pray:

After the kids have formed the Chain of Disciples, **pray:** Dear God, Bless our Chain of Disciples. We're celebrating the words of Jesus: "Follow me and I will make you fish for people." (John 1:17) Amen.

Another Go:

Goldfish crackers make a great snack to go along with this activity. For added fun, serve gingerbread people, too!

PEACE BE TO YOUR HOUSE

Bible Verse: "Peace be to you, and peace be to your house, and peace be to all that you have." (1 Samuel 25:6)

Activity: Kids will visit the home of a member of your congregation.

Materials: Bible

Ready:

Makes plans to have your kids visit the home of a member of your congregation. Let the church member know how long the visit will be and about how many kids and adults will be visiting. Your host may simply chat with the kids, introduce them to family members or pets, share a hobby, and/or give a brief tour of the house and yard. Your host may be happy to serve a snack. If you are visiting someone who might find this difficult, consider bringing a snack along with you.

Arrange transportation if the home is not within safe walking distance. You will want to send a notice to parents several weeks ahead of time, and obtain written permission if this is the policy of your church.

Set:

Remind your host, parents, and kids of the upcoming visit. Collect any permission slips and double check on transportation.

Go!:

Gather the kids together.

Say: Today we are going to visit the home of someone in our church. (Say a word or two about the person.)

Continue: When the Christian faith was organized, before churches were built, Christians met in one another's homes. Open the Bible and read the verse, then have the kids say it with you.

Say: This verse is from the Old Testament. When the early Christians visited one another, they might have said this verse as a greeting or blessing. That's what we're going to do today. We'll say the verse to our host when we visit his/her home.

Have the kids practice saying the verse in their most enthusiastic voices. Explain that when your host opens the door, you will **whisper:** "One, two, three" and then you will all say the verse together. Practice once more right before you leave for the visit.

When you arrive at your host's door, gather the kids together and lead them in saying the verse. Once inside, have kids greet the host, shaking hands or giving hugs as they say their names. Enjoy the visit!

Pray:

Just before you leave, ask all to bow their heads. **Pray:** Dear God, Thank you for the kindness of (host) who has invited us to this lovely home. Peace be to this house. Amen.

Another Go:

Have kids write thank-you notes to the person they visited. Encourage older kids to write a sentence or two describing something they especially enjoyed about the visit. You may want to have kids draw a picture of their own homes or families on their thank-you notes.

KNOCK AND THE DOOR WILL BE OPENED

Bible Verse: "Ask, and it will be given to you; search, and you will find; knock and the door will be opened for you." (Matthew 7:7)

Activity: Kids will go on a scavenger hunt, repeating the verse and gathering items to make door hangers for their rooms at home.

Materials: Bible, foam sheets, scissors, paper, markers, stickers

Ready:

Gather the materials that kids will collect to make the door hangers. Sheets of colored foam (9 inches X 12 inches) can be found in many craft departments. If you cannot locate the foam, posterboard or very heavy paper will work, too. Cut the sheets into 4 1/2 by 12 inch rectangles. Fold over the top third of the 12-inch length. With scissors, make about a two-inch vertical cut. Then fold the length in the other direction and make a one-inch horizontal cut at the midpoint of the first cut. (When unfolded, you will see a cross.) This is the opening for the doorknob. You will need stickers and markers, too.

For the scavenger hunt, kids will go to several locations in the church to collect the craft materials. You will need to station someone at each location to answer their knock on the door, hand out the materials left for them there, and give them a clue as to where to go next. This activity works especially well during the Sunday school hour or when there are other groups meeting at church, but if you

gather at another time, you can simply recruit helpers to be stationed at each location.

Make up clues to get kids from location to location. For instance, if you want them to go to the Senior High Class, you might write: "This will be your class when you are a freshman."

Set:

Give the materials and the clues to the helpers who are assisting you with the scavenger hunt. (Be certain to keep the first clue yourself.) Ask them to please keep the door closed so the kids will need to knock on it. You may also want to give your helpers a copy of the Bible verse or the Scripture reference, so they are ready to prompt the kids if they have trouble repeating the verse.

As kids come into the room, **say:** I'm glad you all came in the door today. I'm so happy to see you!

Go!:

Call the kids together. Open the Bible and read the verse, then have the kids say it with you. Since they will need to say the verse during the scavenger hunt, have them repeat it several times to make certain that they learn it.

Say: This verse was spoken by Jesus. He is telling us that if we want the good things that faith brings to come into our lives, they will. But God wants us to ask for faith, to search for faith, and to knock on doors to find faith.

Ask: Does Jesus really mean to go around and knock on doors to find faith? *(No, it's an expression to help us understand that we must put energy and effort into finding and keeping our faith so that good things will come to us.)*

Explain the scavenger hunt to the kids, telling them that they are to follow clues to each location, knock on the door, and say the verse for the person who opens the door. That person will then give them the clue to the next location and some items. Practice the verse one more time, give kids the first clue, and send them on their way.

When kids return, ask them who they met during the scavenger hunt and what they think they are going to make with the craft materials, then set them to work. Have them write all or part of the verse on their doorknob hanger, then decorate the hanger using the markers and stickers.

Pray:

When the doorknob hangers are finished, tell the kids that when they get home, they are to hang them over the doorknobs to their rooms to help them remember the verse. Next ask kids to close their eyes for a prayer. Ask them to knock three times with you. Then **pray:** Dear God, We know that you love us and want us to find good things through faith. Help us to remember to ask and search and knock. Amen.

Another Go:

Have your kids make festive decorations for the door to your room or any door at church. Consider crepe paper streamers, collages made from old magazine pictures, or designs created on paper plates or white paper. You may want to print the words: " Knock and the door will be opened for you." (Matthew 7:7)

NUMBER ALL MY STEPS

Bible Verse: "Does he not see my ways, and number all my steps?" (Job 31:4)

Activity: Kids will count how many steps it takes to reach a variety of locations around the church.

Materials: Bible, snack (optional)

Ready:

Think about places in your church that your kids might visit, counting their steps along the way. Some locations can be nearby, such as the water fountain and others farther away, such as the choir room, the kitchen, the pastor's study, or locations in the churchyard such as the church. Consider asking your choir director to play the kids a song on the practice piano when they arrive in the choir room or suggest your pastor give the kids a tour of his or her study. You may want to have a snack waiting in the kitchen. (This can be the last location kids visit.)

Older kids will enjoy counting their steps on their own and then comparing numbers. With younger kids, you might want to have everyone start at the same time. Kids can count aloud, with your help if necessary.

Set:

Set up the snack, if you have one, in the kitchen and say a word of reminder to any helpers who will be waiting to greet the kids.

As kids arrive, **say:** I'm so glad you stepped into our room today.

Go!:

Gather the kids together and **ask:** Have you ever counted every step that you took all day long? After the kids respond, **say:** Did you know that God counts each of your steps?

Open the Bible and read the verse, then have the kids say it with you.

Ask: What do you think this verse means? *(That God sees what we do and watches over us.)* How does it make you feel to know that God is watching over you? *(glad, secure)*

Say: God loves us and watches over us. God sees every step that we take! To celebrate this, we're going to count our steps.

Explain how you want the kids to do this (individually or as a group.) Announce the first destination and have them guess ahead of time how many steps they will take. Before they leave, have everyone say the verse together.

When you arrive at the first destination, ask kids how many steps they took and compare that number to the guess. Head off to each destination in the same way, by estimating how many steps and saying the verse.

Pray:

When you have reached your last destination, ask the kids to step softly in place and bow their heads as you **pray**: Dear God, We're glad that you watch over us. We're glad that you see our ways and number all of our steps. Amen.

Serve the snack, if you have one.

Another Go:

Let the kids take turns tracing one another's feet with chalk onto the church sidewalk or with crayon onto a long sheet of paper. Have them write the Bible verse as a border around the footprints.

I HAVE FINISHED THE RACE

Bible Verse: "I have fought the good fight, I have finished the race, I have kept the faith." (2 Timothy 4:7)

Activity: Kids will run the race, say the verse, and be crowned with a laurel wreath.

Materials: Bible, posterboard or craft paper, marker, tape or stapler, green crepe paper streamers, twisted paper, or wide ribbon, basket, yarn, chair

Ready:

When kids finish the race, they will be crowned with a laurel wreath. Create wreaths using crepe paper streamers, twisted paper (available in craft departments), or wide ribbon. Cut lengths to fit the size of your kids' heads (you can get this about right by measuring wreaths a bit smaller than your own head.) Staple or tape the ends together. Place the laurel wreaths in the basket. Write the Bible verse on the posterboard or a large sheet of paper. The race is best held outdoors, but if need be, kids can be asked to racewalk indoors. Kids will race to the Bible verse poster and then back to the starting point.

Set:

Use the yarn to mark the starting point, which is also the finish line. Place the Bible verse poster at the halfway point of the race, taped to a chair. Have the basket off to the side, near the starting point.

Go!:

Gather the kids together. **Ask:** Have you ever run a race? After the kids share their experiences, **say:** Races have been held since ancient times. In fact the Bible even mentions races. Open the Bible and read the verse, then have the kids say it with you.

Say: Paul, who helped spread the news of Jesus, wrote these words in a letter to Timothy, another early Christian. Paul wasn't really talking about a race. He was comparing the effort it takes to run and complete a race to the work he was doing telling others about Jesus.

Ask: Paul said, "I have kept the faith." What did he mean? *(That he had worked hard to help create the early church and not given up even when it was difficult; that he had not lost his belief in Jesus or the importance of telling others about Jesus.)*

Explain that in ancient times, the winners of a race were often crowned with a laurel wreath. The laurel wreath was a symbol of honor and victory. Next tell kids that in honor of Paul they are going to run a race and be crowned with laurel wreaths.

Take kids to the starting point and have them line up behind the yarn. If your group is large, you may want to have two lines. Explain that when it is their turn, they are to run to the Bible verse poster, look at the verse and touch the poster, run back to the starting point and say the verse with the group. The next person in line will crown the runner with a laurel wreath and then start out on the race.

Encourage everyone to cheer on the runners. You can crown the last runner.

Pray:

When all have finished the race, ask them to touch their laurel wreaths and bow their heads. **Pray:** Dear God, We have fought the good fight, we have finished the race, we have kept the faith. Amen.

Another Go:

Let kids try their hand at finger races. Draw starting and finish lines with masking tape and set down some objects for kids to race around using their pointer and middle fingers.

TEACH ME YOUR PATHS

Bible Verse: "Make me to know your ways, O Lord; teach me your paths." (Psalm 25:4)

Activity: Working in pairs, kids will use yarn to create paths

Materials: Bible, yarn

Ready:

Since yarn in skeins often tangles, you may want to wind the yarn into balls. Each pair will need a ball of yarn in a different color.

This activity works best when kids are given a lot of space to create their paths, either throughout the church, a large fellowship hall, or in the churchyard.

Set:

As kids arrive tease them by **saying:** Gosh, I'm so glad you didn't get lost on your way today.

Go!:

Gather the kids together and **ask:** Have you ever really gotten lost? After the kids share their experiences, **say:** Getting lost can be scary. Sometimes we don't know which way to go.

Ask: Now here's another question. Have you ever had to make a really hard decision? After the kids answer this question, **say:** Sometimes it's scary to make a decision. Sometimes we just don't know what to decide.

Open the Bible and read the verse, then have the kids say it with you.

Say: This verse is from Psalm 25. The person who wrote it was asking for God's guidance, especially when life gets scary. If we know God's ways and know how God wants us to live, then we can make good decisions and take the right paths.

Ask: What does it mean to take the right path? *(to do what God wants us to do)* How do we know what God wants us to do? *(by praying and listening for God's guidance; by reading the Bible and understanding what it teaches us; by listening to the advice of our parents, church members, and other Christians)*

Announce that to illustrate the verse, kids will now make yarn paths. Have them pair up. Make certain they know where they may and may not go when they are creating their paths.

After their yarn path is laid out, let each pair walk it, then trade paths with another pair. If time permits have the pairs travel other yarn paths too. When the paths have been traveled, have kids roll up the yarn.

Pray

Ask kids to line up, single file. Have them put their hands on the shoulders of the person in front of them. Then ask them to bow their heads and close their eyes.

Pray: Dear God, We pray that we will know your ways and that you will teach us your paths. Help us to live as you want us to live, to make good decisions, and to travel on the right paths. Amen.

Another Go

For a silly snack, give kids string red licorice. Let them create a path or two on a paper plate before eating the candy.

TWO OR THREE ARE GATHERED

Bible Verse: "For where two or three are gathered in my name, I am there among them." (Matthew 18:20)

Activity: Kids will play a Gathering Game that brings them together in groups of two and three.

Materials: Bible, paper, markers or crayons, scissors, tape, basket, bell or whistle

Ready:

For the Gathering Game, kids will pull symbols from a basket and then go to the matching symbol taped to the floor. Draw simple Christian symbols on 8 1/2 by 11 inch paper. Symbols might include: cross, fish, heart, candle, butterfly, dove, angel, boat, drops of water, coins, shepherd, manger, and shell. Next, cut new sheets of paper into quarters and draw the same symbols. You will need one symbol per child. If your group is large you can repeat symbols but color them in different colors. Put the smaller symbols in a basket.

You may want to use a larger space for this activity.

Set:

Before kids arrive, tape the large symbols to the floor in groups of two and three. When all of the kids have arrived, make certain you have an equal number of symbols and kids. Remove extra symbols from the floor and the basket.

Go!

Call the kids together. **Say:** Today, we're going to begin by playing a Gathering Game. Have the kids each pull a symbol from the basket. Explain that when they hear the bell or whistle, they are to find that symbol on the floor and stand on it.

Give the signal. Once they have reached their symbol spot, **say:** You are now gathered in groups of two and three. And Jesus is right there among you!

Call the kids back together and have them return the smaller symbols to the basket.

Next, open the Bible and read the verse, then have the kids say it with you.

Ask: What do you think this verse means? (that Jesus is with Christians when they meet for prayer, study, worship, and fellowship, even if there are only two or three people present)

Say: Whenever Christians gather, Jesus is there among us in spirit. This is a wonderful thought!

Play the game a few more times. Each time the kids arrive at their new symbol spot, ask them to shake hands with one another and say the verse.

Pray:

Call the kids together. Ask them to form a circle by joining hands or linking elbows. **Pray**: Dear God, We thank you that as Christians we have opportunities to gather together. We remember the promise of Jesus: "Where two or three are gathered in my name, I am there among you." (Matthew 18:20) Amen.

Another Go:

Let kids use shelf or craft paper to create festive tablerunners for your next church luncheon or supper. Have them write "Gathered in His Name" down the center and then decorate the runners with Christian symbols.

Happy Hearts

Bear One Another's Burdens

Bible Verse: "Bear one another's burdens, and in this way you will fulfill the law of Christ." (Galatians 6:2)

Activity: Kids will make Burden Bracelets to wear until they help someone bear a burden.

Materials: Bible, permanent markers, colored plastic report covers, scissors, clear tape, backpack and books

Ready:

Colored plastic report covers are best for this activity but heavier plastic folders will work, too. One folder should yield about eighteen bracelets. With the folder held vertically (as if you are opening it), cut the cover into one-inch strips. When this is done, trim about two inches off the length of each bracelet. Kids will adjust them to fit their own wrists. For younger kids, you may want to write the verse on the bracelets ahead of time.

Fill the backpack with books.

Set:

As kids arrive, ask them to put on the backpack **saying:** Please help me by carrying my burden for a minute or two? It's so heavy! Switch the backpack from child to child, commenting each time on what a heavy burden it is.

Go:

After all the kids have had a turn to wear the backpack, ask them to sit down. **Say:** Thank you so much for helping me carry my burden today. It's so nice when someone helps you with your burdens. In fact, there is even a Bible verse that talks about this.

Open the Bible and read the verse, then have the kids say it with you.

Continue: Sometimes we carry burdens that aren't really heavy objects, but they are problems and responsibilities that are difficult or troubling.

Ask: What might some of those burdens be? *(We need help with our math or reading; we are worried about a bad situation at school and need advice; we are on crutches and can't carry our backpacks; we are sad because our Grandma is very sick.)*

Say: In the Bible verse, Paul is telling Christians that we should help one another by bearing one another's burdens. To help you remember the verse, we're going to make Burden Bracelets. You're to wear your Burden Bracelet until you help someone carry a burden, either a burden of heavy objects or a difficulty or trouble. When you have carried the burden, ask the person you helped to cut off your Burden Bracelet for you.

Give out the bracelets and the markers, instructing kids to write the verse on the bracelet. Have scissors ready for any bracelets that need trimming. Finally, have kids take turns taping the bracelets together on one another's wrists.

Pray:

When the bracelets are secured to wrists, ask kids to touch their bracelets with their other hand as you **pray:** Dear God, We promise to wear our Burden Bracelets until we help someone with a burden. We know that as Christians we are called to bear one another's burdens. Amen.

Another Go:

Perhaps there is a way that kids can help at your church to carry a burden. Check with your pastor or building and grounds committee to see if there are chairs, books, groceries, or other items to be moved or transported.

Done In Love

Bible Verse: "Let all that you do be done in love."
(I Corinthians 16:14)

Activity: Kids will create Anytime Valentines to be delivered any time of the year.

Materials: Bible, paper, glue, scissors, markers, and decorative items such as paper doilies, stickers, lace, ribbon, and/or tissue

Ready:

Kids will especially enjoy creating the valentines at a time of the year other than February. You may want to precut the paper into heart shapes for younger kids.

The valentines can be mailed or delivered to those in your congregation who could use a bit of extra love and cheer such as the sick, shut-in, or elderly.

Set:

Arrange the craft supplies on the table. As the kids arrive, ask them to look at the supplies and try to figure out what they will be making.

Go!:

Gather the kids together and begin.

Say: Who can tell me what we're going to make today? If they have trouble figuring it out, give them a hint such as "Usually we make these in February."

Say: But any time of the year is a good time to show people we love them with a valentine. Today we're making Anytime Valentines in celebration of this Bible verse.

Open the Bible and read the verse, then have the kids say it with you.

Tell the kids who will be receiving the Anytime Valentines. **Say:** And I bet they will be surprised and pleased to receive a valentine in *(say the month)*. Before kids begin, explain that they are to decorate the front of the valentine, and on the back write: "Done in love by" and sign their names. You may want to write this on the classroom board for younger kids.

Pray:

When the valentines are finished, ask the kids to each hold one of their creations. **Pray**: Dear God, Here is one of my Anytime Valentines, done in love, because any time is a good time to do something loving. Amen.

Another Go:

Invite a member of your church to talk with the kids about the various mission projects of your church. The kids can then color pictures that depict these projects. Mount their pictures on posterboard or a bulletin board for others to admire. Label their art with the verse and a brief explanation.

BLESSED ARE THE PEACEMAKERS

Bible Verse: "Blessed are the peacemakers, for they will be called children of God." (Matthew 5:9)

Activity: Kids will practice settling disagreements at their very own Dispute Settlement Center.

Materials: Bible, paper, pen

Ready:

For this activity, you will need to come up with disputes for the kids to settle. Keep in mind the age of your kids as you do this. Address each dispute to the defendant (the person who is accused). The other party mentioned will be the complainant (the person with the complaint). Here are some examples:

- You are being accused of writing on the school walls by the principal.

- Your friend is complaining that you tease him or her every day on the playground.

- Your mother or father is angry and worried because you have taken money from the kitchen change jar without asking.

- The school crossing guard says that you repeatedly run across the crossing when the stop sign is being held up.

- Your neighbor is upset because your dog barks at five a.m. every morning.

Kids will work in groups of three, so you will need one dispute for every three kids. Write each dispute on a separate piece of paper. The disputes can be read to nonreaders.

Set:

As kids arrive, complain about a pretend *(or real dispute)* in your life. You might say: I'm just so upset because Josh refuses to help me with the dishes. I just don't know how to solve this problem.

Go!

When all of the kids have arrived, call them together. **Begin by asking:** When you came in today, I mentioned a dispute going on at my house. Does anyone remember what it is? After the kids respond, **say:** I want peace at my house, but I just don't know how to solve this. Can any of you help me settle my dispute? After the kids respond, thank them for their suggestions, then **say:** As

Christians, we can help one another solve disputes and problems. God wants us to work toward peace.

Open the Bible and read the verse, then have the kids say it with you. Explain that Jesus spoke these words in a sermon now called "The Sermon on the Mount" because it took place on a mountain or a hillside.

Say: As we have been discussing, one of the ways to work for peace is to settle disputes in calm, thoughtful, and loving manners. Many communities have what is called a "dispute settlement center." These are places where people go to work out their disputes against one another instead of going to court. Family, work, and neighborhood disputes are often solved peacefully in this way.

Explain that the kids will now practice working out disputes at a pretend dispute settlement center for kids. Divide them into groups of three and set three chairs in a circle. Begin by calling a group forward to sit in the chairs. Appoint one child to be the peer counselor (who helps mediate the dispute); appoint another child to be the complainant (the person with the complaint); and the last child to be the defendant (the person who is accused of the complaint).

Hand a dispute to the peer counselor, who will read it aloud. Then have the kids carry on a discussion of the dispute, with each one playing his or her role. (You may need to do some prompting to get the discussion going and also to wrap it up.) When the dispute has been solved, have everyone say the Bible verse.

Continue until each group has had a turn to settle a dispute. If you have disputes left, you may want to have the groups take another turn, with the kids in the group switching roles. To conclude, **ask**: How did those of you who served as defendants feel? How did those of you filing complaints feel? How did it feel to be a peer counselor and help settle a dispute?

Pray:

After the kids respond, ask them to join hands in a circle. **Pray:** Dear God, Jesus said, "Blessed are the peacemakers, for they will be called children of God." (Matthew 5:9) As we learn to settle disputes, we know that we are peacemakers. Amen.

Another Go:

Teach kids some favorite songs that speak of peace such as "I've Got Peace Like a River" or "Let There Be Peace on Earth." Tell them that sometimes, when they are angry or upset, it helps to hum or whistle the songs as they think about and pray for a peaceful solution to the problem.

DO TO OTHERS

Bible Verse: "Do to others as you would have them do to you." (Luke 6:31)

Activity: Using paper bag props, kids will come up with situations relating to the Golden Rule.

Materials: Bible, paper bag, props (see Ready)

Ready:

Kids will take turns pulling out a prop from the paper bag. They will then use the prop to help them come up with a situation that goes against the Golden Rule and one that shows living the Golden Rule. For example, someone pulls out a football and says, "An example of going against the Golden Rule is to not invite a new kid in my neighborhood to play football with me. An example of living by the Golden Rule is to invite the new kid and any other kids who might be shy to come and play."

Gather a wide variety of props such as toys, school items, packaged food, clothing, and sports equipment. You will need one item per child. If your group is small, you may want to have several items per child and let kids take a few turns. Place the props in a large paper bag, turning over the sides of the bag so its contents are hidden.

Set:

Have the paper bag in clear view. Greet kids as they arrive, pointing to the paper bag and **saying:** Today we're going to use the contents of that paper bag to talk about living by the Golden Rule.

Go!:

Begin by holding up the paper bag. **Say:** Inside this mysterious paper bag are the props for today's game. But first, here's the Bible verse behind the game.

Open the Bible and read the verse, then have the kids say it with you.

Ask: This verse is so famous that it has a nickname. Does anyone know what that nickname is? *(the Golden Rule)* **Say:** One of the greatest teachings of Jesus was his message of love. This verse tells us that we are to treat others with love. Sometimes, it's not always easy to know exactly how to do that. Jesus gives us a clever tip. Treat others as we want to be treated. This is the Golden Rule.

Tell kids that now it's time to discover the contents of the mystery bag. Explain that when it's their turn, they are to reach a hand into the bag, pull out one item, and look at the item. Then they are to come up with one way that they could use the item to go against the Golden Rule, and one way that they could use the item to live the Golden Rule. You may want to give an example or two before the game begins.

Pray:

When the game is over, ask the kids to bow their heads and close their eyes as you **pray:** Dear God, Jesus said, "Do to others as you would have them do to you." (Matthew 7:12) The Golden Rule is golden indeed. Amen.

Another Go:

Let the kids customize rulers to help them remember the Golden Rule. They may use permanent markers to write the verse (or part of it) on the back of the ruler and/or gold paint pens to decorate it.

LET THE LITTLE CHILDREN COME TO ME

Bible Verse: "But Jesus said, 'Let the little children come to me, and do not stop them; for it is to such as these that the kingdom of heaven belongs.'" (Matthew 19:14)

Activity: Kids will make a flannel board story to share with younger children.

Materials: Bible, flannel board, dryer sheets, markers, a baby picture of yourself

Ready:

Since dryer sheets will adhere to a flannel board, kids will color on the sheets to create the pieces of the flannel board story. You will need at least one sheet per child. Sheets may be ironed lightly to remove creases.

Arrange for your kids to present their flannel board story to a group of younger children. If they can't do this the day the flannel board story is created, they may present it at another time.

One story that works well for this project is the Creation Story. (Genesis 1:1-31) The story can be broken down into these elements of creation: sun, moon, stars, earth, seas, plants, air, sea, and land creatures. Since plants and creatures come in many varieties, kids can make several pieces that illustrate these.

When your kids present the story to the younger children, it may work best if you are the narrator. You may want to practice telling the story very simply.

Set:

As kids arrive, show them the baby picture, asking them to guess who it is. Don't tell them that it is you until everyone has arrived.

Go!:

Call the kids. **Ask:** Who was that darling baby in the picture? After they guess, **say:** Did you know the cute little baby in the picture was me? **Ask:** Are babies important to our church? After the kids respond, spend a few minutes discussing you church's ministry to babies and young children *(Baptism, nursery care, the toddler class)*

Say: Babies and young children are important to our church just as bigger kids are, too. Younger kids are part of our family here at church, and they are part of God's family. Jesus made it very clear that children are important.

Open the Bible and read the verse, then have the kids say it with you.

Next, lead kids in singing "Jesus Loves Me," a beloved song inspired by this verse.

Say: As Christians, it is our job to be kind to younger children and to help them learn about our faith.

Explain the flannel board project, then read the Creation Story from the Bible or tell a simplified version. Assign kids elements of creation to illustrate. Tell them that their pictures will show up best if outlined in a darker color. When the flannel board pieces are finished, have the kids practice putting them on the flannel board as you retell the story.

Pray: Just before your kids set out to present their flannel board story,
pray: Dear God, We're glad that Jesus said, "Let the little children come to me." (Matthew 19:14) Help us to love and care for all the younger kids in our church. Amen.

Another Go: Consider having your kids meet with the younger kids
again from time to time so they can really get to know them. They can create another flannel board story, teach the kids songs with motions, read or share picture books, or invite them to the room for a simple snack.

LIVE AS CHILDREN OF LIGHT

Bible Verse: "For once you were darkness, but now in the Lord you are light. Live as children of light." (Ephesians 5:8)

Activity: After enjoying a flashlight game, kids will donate their flashlights to a local shelter or relief agency.

Materials: Bible, flashlights

Ready:

Shelters and relief agencies welcome donations of flashlights. Send a notice home with kids several weeks ahead of time, asking them to bring in a disposable flashlight or a new flashlight outfitted with batteries. Shelters are glad to have a supply on hand, especially for weather-related emergencies.

You will need a flashlight yourself. Also, you may want to purchase some additional flashlights for kids who come without one.

The flashlight game works best in a darkened room. If you don't have blinds or curtains, you may want to put dark paper or cloth over your windows.

Set:

As kids arrive, **say:** You light up my day! I'm so glad to see you. Have them keep their flashlights with them.

Go!:

Gather the kids together, asking them to please put their flashlights aside for now. **Begin by saying:** Thank you for bringing in flashlights. In just a few minutes, we're going to play a flashlight game, but first listen to a Bible verse about darkness and light.

Open the Bible and read the verse, then have the kids say it with you.

Say: Paul wrote these words in a letter to early Christian believers.

Ask: What do you think Paul means when he tells them that once they were darkness but now they are light? *(When they were darkness they did not know about Jesus and how to live as Christians.)*

Say: When we live as Christians and behave as God wants us to behave, we are children of light. The next verse says, "For the fruit of the light is found in all that is good and right and true."

After giving a few examples, ask each child to tell the group one specific way that kids can behave as children of light. (*I can write a letter to my grandpa who is in a nursing home; I can come to Sunday school and worship; I can donate my used clothes and toys to a shelter; I can be respectful of God's earth by recycling and not wasting water; I can pray for my friend who is sick.*)

Next, tell the kids it's time for the flashlight game. Darken the room. Ask kids to sit in a circle. Explain that you will shine your flashlight on one of them. Then everyone is to shine their flashlights on that person, and that person is to say: Live as children of light!

Pray:

When the game is finished, ask kids to shine their flashlights on the ceiling as you **pray:** Dear God, May we live as children of light. Amen.

Collect the flashlights, explaining to the kids where they will be going and why they are needed.

Another Go:

At another time, you may want to collect birthday candles for a shelter. Remind your kids that even children in difficult circumstances want to have candles to blow out on their birthdays. Serve a snack with candles to add to the fun and let everyone help blow them out after saying: Live as children of light.

STRIVING SIDE BY SIDE

Bible Verse: "I will know that you are standing firm in one spirit, striving side by side with one mind for the faith of the gospel." Philippians 1:27b

Activity: Kids will provide a gift wrap service for the congregation.

Materials: Bible, gift wrap, self-stick bows, gift tags, pens, scissors, tape

Ready:

If your church collects gifts at Christmas to donate to a needy family or a local shelter or relief agency, kids can provide a gift wrap service to wrap those gifts. Announce to your congregation ahead of time when the gifts will be wrapped.

If your church does not collect gifts at Christmas, consider having the kids provide the service anyway, with church members bringing in any gifts they would like wrapped. You may want to put out a jar and ask for small donations in exchange for the service. The money can be used for a cause your church supports at Christmas.

The kids will need plenty of table space for working, especially if your group is large.

Set:

The wrapping will go best if it is done assembly-line style. Kids can team up with a partner, with one team unrolling and cutting the paper; the second team wrapping and taping; and the third team sticking on bows and gift tags. Depending on the number of kids, you can form one or more assembly lines.

Set out the supplies.

Go!

Begin by asking: Does anyone know what it means to "strive side by side?" *(to work together)* **Say:** Here's a Bible verse that uses that very expression.

Open the Bible and read the verse, then have the kids say it with you.

Say: Today we are going to strive side by side for the faith. Explain the gift wrap service and the cause it is supporting. Then welcome those who have brought gifts to be wrapped and let the assembly line roll!

Pray:

When all of the gifts have been wrapped, ask everyone to bow their heads and close their eyes. **Pray:** Dear God, We pray that these gifts will help bring the spirit of Christmas to those who receive them. Today, we were happy to wrap presents and to strive side by side for the faith of the gospel. Amen.

Another Go:

There may be other ways that your kids can work together to help with Christmas donations at your church, perhaps creating and decorating an Angel Tree or assisting with the delivery of the gifts to the families, agency, or shelter.

DO NOT BE WEARY

Bible Verse: "Brothers and sisters, do not be weary in doing what is right." (2 Thessalonians 3:13)

Activity: To surprise people they catch doing right, kids will make Right Rewards.

Materials: Bible, paper, scissors, markers, stickers, wrapped hard candy

Ready:

Make a sample Right Reward to show the kids. Trim 8 1/2 by 11 inch paper to form a square. **Write:** "Thanks for doing what is right! Love, *(your name)*" on the square and decorate it with stickers and drawings. Next, fold in each of the four corners to the center (with the decorated side now hidden by the folds). Drop a hard candy inside. Secure and seal the Right Reward with a sticker in the center.

Depending on the age of your kids, plan on each child making from two to four Right Rewards. Precut the paper into squares. Beginning writers may simply write the word "Thanks" inside their squares and sign their names, or you can go ahead and write the longer message for them ahead of time.

Set:

As kids come in, say to each one: I caught you doing right! You came to church today. Here's a small reward. Give them a candy.

Go!:

When everyone has arrived, gather the kids together and begin. **Say:** As Christians, we are called to do what is right. Listen to this verse.

Open the Bible and read the verse, then have the kids say it with you.

Continue: Paul gave this advice in a letter to early Christians, but it's good advice for today, too. **Ask:** What are some of the ways that we do what is right? *(help others; tell the truth; give generously; share)* Then **ask:** Do you ever get tired of doing right? After the kids respond, **say:** Although we know that as Christians we are called to do what is right, sometimes it takes a lot of time and energy. Sometimes, we can get weary or tired of doing what is right. That's when it's nice to get encouragement.

Explain that the kids are now going to make Right Rewards to surprise people they catch doing something right. Show kids the sample by removing the sticker and letting them see the words, decorations, and candy inside. Next, set them to work making their own Right Rewards. When the Right Rewards are finished, tell the kids that they should keep their eyes open for folks who are doing right, and surprise them with a Right Reward.

Pray:

Have kids bow their heads and close their eyes. **Pray:** Dear God, May we remember the words of Paul: "Brothers and sisters, do not be weary in doing what is right." Amen.

Another Go:

Let your kids choose a project that will enable them do right. Consider a sock or mitten drive, a church clean up, a canned food collection, or a car wash or bake sale to raise money for a local shelter or other charity that your church supports.

Joyful Voices

LOVE THE LORD YOUR GOD

Bible Verse: "You shall love the Lord your God with all your heart, and with all your soul, and with all your might." (Deuteronomy 6:5)

Activity: After saying the verse in their most exuberant voices, kids will learn to say some of the words in sign language.

Materials: Bible

Ready:

Kids will learn to sign the words for "love," "God," "heart," "soul," and "might" using American Sign Language. Practice signing the words yourself so you can teach them more easily to the kids.

Love: Both hands crossed over heart

God: Right hand raised from elbow, parallel to head

Heart: Right hand with middle finger curled in, hand resting on heart

Soul: Fingers of left hand touch thumb to form "O." Thumb and index finger of right hand touching, reach into "O," and then move upward

Might (Strength): Right fist pulled toward shoulder

If you have someone in your congregation who knows sign language, you may want to invite him or her to come to your class and sign for the kids. Perhaps your guest could sign some of the Bible verses kids have learned through this book!

Set:

Greet kids with the American Sign Language sign for "Welcome." (Bring your open right hand toward your body, keeping palm facing up.) As you do this, offer a word of explanation such as: I'm saying "welcome" to you today with American Sign Language.

Go!

Gather the kids together. Open the Bible and read the verse, then ask the kids to say it with you. Since they will need to know the verse in the upcoming activity, you may want to have them practice saying it several times.

Ask: What are some of the ways that we can love God with all of our heart and all of our soul and all of our might? *(pray often; read the Bible; obey God's laws; participate in Sunday school, worship, and other church activities; show love and compassion to others)*

Say: Let's express the idea of loving God with all of our heart and soul and might by saying the verse in our most exuberant joyful voices.

Divide the group in half and line kids up facing one another. Explain that each side will say a word of the verse, going back and forth until the entire verse has been said. Point to the side that will begin. Lead kids in doing this, encouraging them to use their most expressive and enthusiastic voices. Have kids say the verse again, this time beginning with the other side.

Gather kids back together. **Say:** You did a wonderful job and I certainly could hear you! But people who cannot hear with their ears, listen to words in another way. They listen with sign language.

Ask kids if they know any sign language. After they have shown you some of the sign language they may have learned, teach them to sign the words from the verse listed above. Next, have them sign the words they have just learned as you say the verse. You may want to repeat this several times.

Pray:

Ask kids to form a circle and hold hands. Explain that during the prayer you will send a squeeze around the circle starting with someone on the right or left. Each person will pass it on until it returns to you. Ask kids to bow their heads and close their eyes. **Pray:** Dear God, We will love you with all of our heart *(send squeeze)*, all of our soul *(send squeeze)*, and all of our might *(send squeeze)*. Amen.

Another Go:

Teach kids the sign for "I love you." Thumb, pointer finger, and little finger of the right hand held straight up and the other two fingers curled down. Encourage them to use the sign in the coming weeks to say "I love you" in a brand new way.

SING A NEW SONG

Bible Verse: "O sing to the Lord a new song; sing to the Lord all the earth." (Psalm 96:1)

Activity: Kids will write brand new songs to God.

Materials: Bible, paper and pens or pencils (optional), Christian music and player, rhythm instruments and/or bells (optional)

Ready:

Kids will work in groups of two or three to write their new songs. The tunes of "Twinkle, Twinkle Little Star" and "Row, Row, Row Your Boat" work well for this activity, but you may want to encourage kids to use other tunes or to make up their own. If you have older kids, offer them pens and paper to write down their lyrics. While not necessary, rhythm instruments and bells add to the fun when kids perform their songs.

Set:

As kids arrive, have the music playing.

Go!

Turn off the music and gather the kids together. **Say:** As you came in today, you heard songs that praise God. Have kids tell you any songs they recognized. Next ask them to say the names of some of their favorite Christian songs and hymns.

Say: Since Old Testament times, people have shown their love to God by singing songs of praise and thanksgiving. At one time every single song we sing as Christians, from an old hymn to a Christian rock tune, was a brand new song. Listen to a Bible verse that talks about singing a new song to God.

Open the Bible and read the verse, then have the kids say it with you. (Consider reading the entire psalm to older kids or giving them Bibles and asking them to read it in unison.)

Say: Writing and singing new songs of praise and thanksgiving to God is a way of showing God our love. That's what you're going to do right now!

Divide the kids into groups. Explain that they should first talk about what they want to say in their song of praise, then form the ideas into words that fit a tune. Each group should practice singing the new song several times since they will be performing it when everyone is finished. If you have rhythm instruments or bells, make them available.

When kids seem ready to perform their songs, call them back together. Praise each brand new song with smiles, words, and clapping.

Pray:

Tell the kids that in honor of their brand new songs, you are going to sing the prayer. **Pray:** *(to the tune of "Row, Row, Row Your Boat")* Sing, sing, sing new songs, we sing new songs of praise. Thank you, God, for songs and fun, and the joy of all our days. Amen.

Another Go:

Your church library may have a book that gives the history behind beloved hymns. Share the history of the hymn with your kids before leading them in singing each hymn. If you don't have a book of histories, open your hymnal and show kids the dates their favorite hymns were written and point out who wrote the lyrics and tune.

GO TO THE HOUSE OF THE LORD

Bible Verse: "I was glad when they said to me, "Let us go to the house of the Lord!" (Psalm 122:1)

Activity: Kids will create paper plate portraits to use in a Call to Worship.

Materials: Bible, paper plates, markers or crayons, tape, scissors, yarn

Ready:

Check with your pastor to find a time when your kids may take part in a Call to Worship. If this isn't practical consider having them hold their portraits as they greet worshipers and say the verse before a worship service.

Kids will tape yarn to the plates to create hair. You may want to cut the yarn (red, yellow, black, and brown) into smaller lengths ahead of time.

As a sample, make a paper plate portrait of yourself with your happiest smile.

Set:

As kids come into the room, smile at them and then **say:** I am so glad you are here in God's house.

Go!:

Gather everyone together. **Ask:** Do you like to come to our church? Why? Hopefully the kids will say that they like coming to church. If some of the responses are negative, allow the kids to express their feelings and encourage discussion.

Then say: God wants us to be happy when we come to church. There is even a Bible verse that expresses this happiness.

Open the Bible and read the verse, then have the kids say it with you.

Explain that they are going to say the verse for the congregation as a Call to Worship. Tell the kids when they will do this and how it will be done.

Then say: We're going to surprise the congregation by hiding paper plate portraits behind our backs and holding them up as soon as we start to say the verse.

Show the kids the paper plate portrait you made of yourself, then have them make their own smiling faces.

When the paper plate portraits are finished, admire them. Next, have the kids line up, with their portraits hidden behind their backs. Tell them that when they say the first word of the verse, they are to bring out their portraits and hold them high above their heads. Practice this several times, encouraging them to say the verse slowly and with great enthusiasm.

Give any further instructions about how your kids will present the Call to Worship. If you are presenting the Call to Worship another week, rehearse again before the service begins.

Pray:

Have kids put their paper plate portraits down, and ask them to smile their biggest smiles as they close their eyes and bow their heads. **Pray:** Dear God, I was glad when they said unto me, "Let us go to the house of the Lord!" Thank you for our church. Amen.

Another Go:

Kids will have fun squirting canned cheese onto rice cakes to create happy faces.

Good News of Great Joy

Bible Verse: "But the angel said to them, 'Do not be afraid; for see—I am bringing you good news of great joy for all the people.'" (Luke 2:10)

Activity: To celebrate the joyful news of the angel, kids will play Name That Carol.

Materials: Christmas music and player, songbooks, song sheets, or hymnals *(optional)*

Ready:

During Name That Carol, kids will listen to just a few notes of a carol, then guess what carol it is. Plan on having kids identify and then sing at least four or five carols. Readers may appreciate song sheets, songbooks, or hymnals. Instead of using a player and recorded music, you may have someone in your congregation who can play the carols on the piano, guitar, or other instrument.

Kids will enjoy this activity any time of the year, not just during Advent. They like to sing Christmas carols all year round!

Set:

As kids arrive, have the recorded music or the guest musician, playing Christmas carols.

Go!:

When everyone has arrived stop the music and begin by reading The Christmas Story (Luke 2: 1-20) from the Bible. Then **ask:** What story did I just read? *(the story of the birth of Jesus; the Christmas Story)*

Next read the Bible verse, then have the kids say it with you.

Ask: Why did the angel say, "I am bringing you good news of great joy?" *(Because Jesus is God's son. He came to save us from our sins and offer us eternal life. This was and is good news!)*

Continue: The angel was the first to bring this good news to the shepherds. Today, over two thousand years later, we celebrate the good news of the birth of Jesus during Advent and Christmas. One of the ways we do this is by singing Christmas carols. And to make sure you haven't forgotten your carols, we're going to play Name That Carol.

Play just a few notes of the carol and ask kids to guess which carol it is. If they have trouble, play a few more notes until they recognize the tune. Then lead them in singing the carol.

Pray:

When the singing is finished, **pray:** Dear God, We thank you for carols and we thank you for Christmas. We thank you for Jesus, who was and is good news of great joy for all the people. Amen.

Another Go:

Read a favorite Christmas picture book.

THE WORDS OF MY MOUTH

Bible Verse: "Let the words of my mouth and the meditation of my heart be acceptable to you, O Lord, my rock and my redeemer." (Psalm 19:14)

Activity: After meditating on what they will say, kids will speak kind and encouraging words to one another.

Materials: Bible, rocks, permanent markers, basket or box

Ready:

Since kids will write their names on the rocks, you will need rocks that have a suitable surface for this. You may be able to find enough rocks in your own yard or in your collection of beach or lake stones. If not, many garden supply shops sell rocks at reasonable prices.

Set:

As kids arrive, have them each choose a rock and write her or his name on it.

Go!

When all of the kids have written their names on a rock, ask them to sit down and hold their rocks in their hands. **Say:** I hope that you all like your personalized rocks! There are verses in the Bible that speak of God being our rock. Here's one of them.

Open the Bible and read the verse, then have the kids say it with you.

Ask: How is God's love like a rock? *(God's love never changes; God is forever, strong, and sturdy like a rock.)* **Say:** In the Bible, the rock is a symbol of God.

Say the verse again.

Continue: This verse is a prayer asking God to help us make the meditations of our hearts, which are our thoughts, and the words that we speak, acceptable to God. One of the ways that we can do this is to think good thoughts about others and then to share those good thoughts by speaking kind and encouraging words to them.

Have the kids put their rocks in the basket or box. Shake it, then ask each child to each pick out a new rock. (If they get their own name, they will need to trade with someone else.)

Say: I want you to meditate or think about the person whose name you just received. In a minute I will ask you to say kind and encouraging words to that person.

After kids have had a minute or two to meditate, have them, one at a time, say the name of the person on the rock they chose, look at that person, and say a few kind and encouraging words to him or her. When they are finished speaking, they should return the rock to its owner.

Pray:

Ask kids to hold their rocks tightly in their fist while you **pray:** Dear God, Let the words of our mouths and the meditations of our hearts be acceptable to you, O Lord, our rock and our redeemer. Amen.

Invite kids to take their rocks home with them.

Another Go:

Let kids concoct a rocky snack by stirring candies such as M and M's into pudding or vanilla yogurt.

FOR THE LORD IS GOOD

Bible Verse: "O give thanks to the Lord, for he is good; for his steadfast love endures forever." (Psalm 107:1)

Activity: Kids will work together to write a responsive Prayer of Thanksgiving.

Materials: Bible, posterboard or craft paper, marker

Ready:

Kids will take turns naming ways that they can feel and see God's steadfast love. Those ideas will then form a prayer, with the Bible verse as the response. You may want to ask your pastor if the prayer can be used in an upcoming worship service. Kids will appreciate seeing the prayer they wrote printed in the bulletin.

Set:

As kids arrive, greet each one by **saying:** The Lord is good. It's so nice to see you (name).

Go!

Gather the kids together. **Say:** When you came in today, I greeted you with part of a Bible verse. **Ask:** Do you remember what I said? After the kids respond, open the Bible and read the verse, then have the kids say it with you.

Ask: Do you know what is means to be steadfast? *(to be firmly fixed in place; to be loyal; to be faithful)*

Say: God's love is forever. The Bible verse tells us that we should give thanks to the Lord for his good, steadfast, forever love. Today, we're going to write a Prayer of Thanksgiving to celebrate this love. I'm going to ask you to tell me ways that God shows love to us. We'll write down your ideas and make them part of our prayer.

Bring out the posterboard or craft paper and marker. If you have older kids, appoint one to be the recorder. If not, you can do the job. Let kids take turns contributing ideas for the prayer such as: "You always hear our prayers;" "You watch over us;" "You gave us families to care for us;" "You sent Jesus to teach us;" "You created the earth and everything in it." You may need to help kids rephrase some of their ideas.

Pray:

When the ideas have been recorded, tell the kids that now you will use them in the Prayer of Thanksgiving. Explain that after each line of the prayer, you will pause and the kids will respond with the Bible verse. **Pray:** Dear God, Thank you for your steadfast love. Read the ideas the kids presented, pausing after each line for the kids to respond with the Bible verse. Conclude the prayer with Amen.

Another Go:

Play Circle the Verse. Have kids stand in a circle. The first person says the first word of the Bible verse; the second person the second word; and so on until the verse has been said. After the verse goes around the circle, have kids say it a few more times, getting faster and faster each time.

MY SHEEP HEAR MY VOICE

Bible Verse: "My sheep hear my voice. I know them, and they follow me." (John 10:27)

Activity: During this listening game, kids will identify the voices of one another.

Materials: Bible, toy sheep, sheep figurine, or picture of a sheep, tape recorder and recording tape (optional)

Ready:

For added fun, consider taping your pastor and some members of your congregation saying the Bible verse. If you have time, tape five to ten people, but two or three voices will be sufficient.

Set:

Put the sheep where it can be seen as kids come into the room.

Go!

After all have arrived, hold up the sheep and **say,** "What sound does this animal make?" *(Baaaaaa.)* Ask everyone to say "Baaa" together in their most sheeplike voices.

Say: That's the sound that sheep make. When we hear that sound, we know that we are hearing sheep. But did you know that sheep can recognize the voice of their shepherd? There is a verse in the Bible that refers to this.

Open the Bible and read the verse, then have the kids say it with you.

Say: Jesus called himself "The Good Shepherd." He knew that those who believed in him would follow him, just as sheep follow their shepherds. By believing in Jesus and following his teachings, we are his sheep hearing his voice. To celebrate this idea, we're going to play a listening game.

Have kids spread out through the room. Explain that they are to close their eyes and cover them with their hands. You will tap someone on the shoulder and that person will say: Follow me. With their eyes still closed, kids should raise their hands, and you will call on someone to identify the voice.

Play the game until everyone has had a chance to say, "Follow me."

If you have made a tape of others in your congregation saying the Bible verse, play it now and let kids guess those voices.

Pray:

Ask each child to say Amen in turn around the circle so that once again, everyone can appreciate the qualities of one another's voices. **Pray:** Dear God, Jesus said, "My sheep hear my voice. I know them, and they follow me." (John 10:27) We're glad for the words of Jesus, and we're glad that we can follow him. Amen.

Another Go:

Surprise your kids by telephoning them in the coming week, **saying:** I just wanted to hear the sound of your voice. Kids can be shy with adults on the telephone, so be prepared to ask them a few lively questions and perhaps say a word or two about an upcoming activity you are planning that they will enjoy.

A JOYFUL NOISE TO THE LORD

Bible Verse: "Make a joyful noise to the Lord, all the earth." (Psalm 100:1)

Activity: Joyful Noisemakers and their own creative voices help kids make a joyful noise to the Lord.

Materials: Bible, party noisemakers, other musical instruments *(optional)*

Ready:

Purchase party noisemakers, usually available in packs of six.

Set:

As kids come into the room, greet them in a joyful voice with happy words such as "Hooray, Jamal's here!" and "Yes! Yes! Yes! I'm so glad to see you Maria!" Toot on one of the noisemakers or use whistles, bells, cymbals, or other festive instruments to create joyful noises.

Go!:

After you have greeted all of the kids with joyful noises, **say:** You probably thought that I was acting very silly when I greeted you. But it was fun! I was so happy to see you that I greeted you with joyful noise. There is a verse in the Bible that talks about making a joyful noise to God.

Open the Bible and read the verse, then have the kids say it with you.

Ask: When you are happy, what are some of the joyful noises that you like to make with your voices? After kids share their favorite expressions of happiness, explain that God enjoys hearing joyful voices of happiness, too. Ask them to make their joyful noises all together on the count of three.

Say: And it's fun to praise God with musical instruments that make joyful noises, too. Hand out the Joyful Noisemakers. Then have the kids blow their Joyful Noisemakers on the count of three.

Say: Sometimes when we praise God, we pray quietly or silently. But other times, just as the Bible says, we can praise God with exuberant joyful noises.

Pray:

Explain that during the prayer, on the count of three, kids are to make joyful noises with their voices. Then, when they hear the count again, they are to make joyful noises with their noisemakers. **Pray:** Dear God, We love you and thank you for all of the wonders of this earth. As the psalm says, we will make joyful noises of praise to you. First with our voices: one, two, three (voices) and now with our Joyful Noisemakers: One, two, three (noisemakers.) Amen.

Another Go:

Invite a guest musician to your classroom to make a joyful noise to the Lord, perhaps playing hymns or Christian songs that the kids know. After the musician finishes, encourage kids to ask questions about the musical instrument.

Tempted Taste Buds

Our Daily Bread

Bible Verse: "Give us this day our daily bread." (Matthew 6:11)

Activity: Kids will make and bake crackers, then pray the Lord's Prayer.

Materials: Bible, two baking sheets, timer, potholders, forks, measuring cups and spoons, mixing bowl, 1 1/2 cups of milk or water, 5 cups flour, 1/3 cup oil or melted butter, 1 egg, 2 teaspoons salt

Ready:

For this activity, you will need access to an oven.

Gather the materials needed for the baking adventure. Each child will need a fork.

Set:

Place the equipment and ingredients on the table where the kids will work. Preheat the oven to 400 degrees.

As kids arrive, have them wash their hands, then welcome them to the table.

Go!:

Open the Bible and read the verse, then have the kids say it with you.

Say: This verse is part of a prayer that Jesus taught his disciples called "The Lord's Prayer." The prayer asks God to "give us this day our daily bread," which means "give us something to eat each day." In Bible times, people usually baked fresh bread daily. Sometimes this bread was baked with a rising ingredient, such as yeast, to form loaves or buns. Other times, the riser was not used, in order to make flat bread or crackers. Today, we'll make and bake crackers as our daily bread.

Begin by asking the kids to help measure and pour the liquid ingredients into the mixing bowl. Have someone stir gently with a fork. Add the salt and one cup of the flour, asking someone else to take a turn stirring. Add three more cups of flour, one at a time, with kids stirring the mixture between each addition. Add up to one-half cup more flour if needed to make the dough less sticky. Dough should begin to pull away from the sides of the bowl and form a ball.

Use remaining one-half cup flour to sprinkle on the baking sheets and an area of the table where you will turn the dough.

Place the dough on the floured work area and roll it once in the flour to reduce stickiness. Next, divide the dough in half with your hands, then divide each half again, so you have four fairly equal pieces. Each dough piece will now be divided according to how many kids are present: if you have 8 kids or less, divide each piece in half; 12 kids or less, divide the pieces in thirds; 16 kids or less divide the pieces into fourths. (Even when the dough is divided into sixteenths, it still yields a nice sized cracker.)

Roll the pieces lightly in the flour of the work area, then hand a dough ball to each child. Invite the kids to place their dough on either of two baking sheets, then pat their dough until it is flat. The thinner the dough, the crisper the cracker will be. Kids might need to take turns at the baking sheets to give each other enough elbow room.

Have kids prick their initials into their crackers with the forks. Place the baking sheets into the hot oven, setting the timer for 12 minutes.

Pray:

While the crackers are baking, open the Bible and read Matthew 6:9-13. Then ask the kids to bow their heads and repeat each verse of the prayer after you. Then **pray:** Dear God, Thank you for this prayer and for our delicious daily bread. Amen.

When the timer rings, check on the crackers. If they are turning golden brown at the edges, they're done. If not, let them bake a few more minutes. Remove them from the oven with potholders and allow to cool a bit.

Place warm crackers on napkins and enjoy.

Another Go:

Introduce kids to some of the world's delicious breads such as Russian Black Bread, Irish Soda Bread, and Croissants.

ALL GOOD THINGS

Bible Verse: "Those who are taught the word must share in all good things with their teacher." (Galatians 6:6)

Activity: The teacher will share a good treat and a Bible story with the kids.

Materials: Bible, Bible story book, an apple, box of graham cracker crumbs, apple pie filling, caramel sauce, one container whipping cream or non-dairy whipped topping, cups, serving bowl, serving spoons, spoons, knife, napkins

Ready:

Purchase a large beautiful apple for the opening activity as well as the ingredients for the Caramel Apple Cups. One 21 ounce can of pie filling will serve eight kids. Also, purchasing caramel sauce in a squeeze bottle will create less mess.

At the end of the activity, you will read the kids a Bible story. Find a story they will like in a Bible storybook or picture book.

Set:

Pour filling and crumbs into serving bowls. Unseal the containers of caramel sauce and the whipped topping. Place these ingredients for the Caramel Apple Cups on a table along with cups, spoons, and napkins.

As kids arrive, use the knife to cut the apple into slices onto a napkin. **Say:** Yum! This apple is so good I want to share it with you. Offer apple slices and continue talking about sharing the good apple.

Go!:

When all of the kids have arrived, gather them together. **Say:** What do you learn by coming to church? *(We learn about God, Jesus, the Bible, our faith.)* Who do you learn these things from? *(teachers, leaders, our pastor)*

Say: When you come to church, you are taught God's word and as students of God's word, you share in all good things with your teachers.

Open the Bible and read the verse, then have the kids say it with you.

Continue: Teachers have many good things to share with their students such as Bible stories, craft projects, games, songs, prayers, and snacks. Today I shared my delicious apple with you, and now I'm going to share another fun snack, Caramel Apple Cups. I chose to make my snacks apples because for some reason, apples and teachers just seem to go together!

Have kids wash their hands, then explain how to make the Caramel Apple Cups. First, kids will ladle a serving spoonful of graham cracker crumbs into their cups. Then they will squirt caramel sauce over the crumbs. Next, kids will scoop a large dollop of apple pie filling onto the crumbs and garnish the apples with a squirt or a spoonful of whipped topping. Kids may finish the treat with a sprinkling of crumbs or a swirl of caramel.

Tell kids that you are happy to share this treat with them and that you will also share a Bible story with them while they eat.

Read the Bible story you have chosen.

Pray: Invite the kids to come and offer you a hug, and as they do, put your arms around as many of them as you can. **Pray:** Dear God, We thank you for your word and for all the good things we can share with each other. Amen.

Another Go: Many kids enjoy playing "school" and being the teacher. See if there are any leftover or used curriculum resources at your church that you can share. Old posters, flannel graphs, and games are favorite take home treasures.

INTO THE ARK

Bible Verse: "Two and two, male and female, went into the ark with Noah, as God had commanded Noah." (Genesis 7:9)

Activity: Kids will construct edible arks, then board an assortment of animal crackers two by two.

Materials: Bible, large box or bag of animal crackers, sandwich bread, small jars of peanut butter/and or marshmallow fluff, knives, paper plates, napkins, toy that makes animal sounds (optional). Because many people are allergic to peanuts, you may wish to err on the side of safety and use the marshmallow fluff.

Ready:

You will need three slices of bread per child. Select bread that has a firm texture so the slices will not compress or tear readily as the kids handle them. Consider using plastic knives since they are smaller than metal flatware and may be easier for the kids to use.

Create a sample ark according to the directions in "Go!"

Try to locate a "See and Say" or other toy that makes animal sounds.

Set:

Around the table, place a paper plate for each child topped with three slices of bread. Put knives and the jars of peanut butter and/or marshmallow fluff within easy reach. Have the animal crackers handy.

As kids arrive, invite them to use the toy to fill the room with a variety of animal sounds.

Go!:

Begin by holding up the toy. **Ask:** Do you think the animals you just heard were on Noah's ark? *(Yes)* What other animals might have floated on the ark? *(camels, doves, tigers)* Can you make animal sounds? On the count of three, let's make the sounds together. After the kids respond, **say:** I bet it was noisy on the ark!

Next, ask kids to wash their hands. When this is done, have them take their places at the table in front of the paper plates. Explain that now they will build their own arks and fill them with animals.

Instruct kids to take one slice of bread and spread it with peanut butter and/or marshmallow fluff, then place another slice of bread on top. This is the ark base. Form the prow of the ark by cutting away the corners of the rounded edge of the bread, slicing in an inverted V shape. Set these corner pieces aside–do not eat! Trim away the remaining crusts from the sandwich to use later.

To make the house of the ark, direct kids to cut their last bread slice into four quarter squares of a fairly equal size. Stack these quarter squares one on top of the other, joining them together with peanut butter and/or marshmallow fluff.

Cover the top of the ark base and the ark house with more peanut butter or marshmallow fluff. Place the ark house in the center of the ark base. Top the ark house with the corner pieces to create a roof

Complete the project by having the kids load the deck of the ark with animal crackers and trim the deck with the cut-off crusts for deck railing.

Admire the ark creations; lead the kids in saying the verse; and perhaps in another chorus of animal sounds.

Pray:

Ask kids to bow their heads. **Pray:** Dear God, We are glad for the amazing animals that you saved from the flood, two by two, male and female. Amen.

Invite the kids to make a feast of their arks.

Another Go:

Sing these new words to the tune of "Row, Row, Your Boat": "Load, load, load the ark, before the rains can come, floating, floating, floating, floating 'til the flood is done."

THE GREATEST

Bible Verse: "And now faith, hope, and love abide, these three; and the greatest of these is love." (1 Corinthians 13:13)

Activity: Understanding the meaning of "the greatest" and baking a big heart-shaped cookie, will help kids grasp the importance of love.

Materials: Bible, a variety of objects that can show graduated size, sugar cookie dough, three small tubes of different colored frosting, baking sheet, aluminum foil, plastic wrap, timer, potholders, knife, napkins

Ready:

Gather three each of several kinds of objects that show graduated size such as measuring cups, buttons, potatoes, or blocks for the opening activity.

You will need access to an oven for the baking activity. Purchase refrigerated cookie dough or make your own. If your group is large, you may want to make two cookies. One cookie will make about twenty servings.

Set:

Cover baking sheet with foil. Leave the dough out of the refrigerator so that it will warm up a bit. Preheat oven according to recipe or package directions.

Place the sets of graduated objects on the table. As the kids come in, invite them to show you which of the like objects is the greatest in size.

Go!:

Gather the kids together and direct them to hold up the objects that they determined were the greatest.

Ask: Now that you have shown me which objects are greatest in size, can you describe for me the people who are your greatest friends? (Go round robin through the group.)

Say: What makes a friend one of your greatest friends is not just how funny or talented that friend is; it's most likely how much that friend loves you and how much you love him or her.

Continue: In the same way, a cartoon hero, such as Superman, is not the greatest because he is strong, bulletproof, and able to fly. He is the greatest because he does super acts out of his love for people.

Then say: What makes Jesus the greatest real person ever isn't just his powers to calm a storm, heal sick people, or raise the dead. What makes Jesus the greatest is his love for all of us. Listen to this verse in the Bible that talks about the importance of love.

Open the Bible and read the verse, then have the kids say it with you.

Say: Faith and hope without love are not great by themselves. For example, faith in Jesus without love for your neighbor is not a great faith. Hope in going to heaven without loving God is not a great hope. Love must come first and be the greatest: love for God, our neighbors, our families, and ourselves.

Have the kids wash their hands as you put the dough on the baking sheet. Lay a sheet of plastic wrap over the dough. This will enable the kids to work without the dough sticking to their hands.

Invite the kids to take turns or work as a group to fashion one big heart-shaped cookie. The cookie should be a fairly consistent thickness.

Slide the cookie into the oven and set the timer for twelve minutes. Check on the cookie, removing when the edges are just beginning to brown. While the cookie is baking and cooling, ask kids some questions about other greatest things or people in their lives.

Bring the cookie and frosting to the table. Invite kids to take turns decorating the cookie with the frosting, making two small hearts labeled "faith" and "hope." Then, have them write "love" in giant letters and decorate the rest of the cookie.

Pray:

Before you serve the cookie, **pray:** Dear God, May we have faith, hope, and love, and remember that the greatest of these is love. Amen.

Use the knife to cut the cookie into pieces for the kids to enjoy.

Another Go:

Have kids each make a heart garland by cutting out paper hearts and taping them together. On each heart, they can write the name of one of their great friends.

TASTE AND SEE

Bible Verse: "O taste and see that the Lord is good; happy are those who take refuge in him." (Psalm 34:8)

Activity: Kids will associate the taste of sweetness with reading the Bible, then assemble candy bookworms as enticement to read more.

Materials: Bibles, candy, tape, permanent markers

Ready:

You will need several bags of individually wrapped candies with twist ends such as mints, taffy, and sour balls. Kids will tape the twist ends together to fashion their bookworms, so have plenty of tape dispensers. Markers will be used to color in eyes.

Set:

Have the bookworm supplies nearby as well as one piece of candy per child for immediate use.

Place Bibles around the table so that each child, even nonreaders, may participate.

As kids arrive, help them to locate Genesis 1:1.

Go!:

Ask everyone to point a finger at the first word in the Bible, then challenge the group to read that word together on the count of three. As soon as this happens, quickly give everyone a piece of candy, with instructions to open and enjoy it immediately.

Ask: What one word best describes the taste of candy? *(sweet)* Why do we like the taste of candy so much? *(because it's good!)* **Say:** Today, when you read the first word of the Bible, I instantly gave you a taste of something sweet. This idea comes from a Jewish custom. When a Jewish child reads the first word of the Torah, the Jewish Bible, the child receives a piece of candy. The child sees God's word and tastes the sweetness at the same time. This custom helps children link and remember the candy's good taste with the goodness of God and God's word. Maybe the custom was inspired by this verse from Psalms.

Open the Bible and read the verse, then have the kids say it with you.

Next, explain that they will make candy bookworms to help them remember the goodness of God's word.

Pour out the bags of candy onto the table and put out the tape dispensers and markers. Show kids how to assemble a bookworm by overlapping the twist ends

of two candies, then wrapping the ends together with a short length of tape. When seven candies have been joined in this way, draw eyes with a marker on a piece of candy at one end of the worm.

Help kids as needed and allow them to make as many bookworms as time and supplies permit. Explain that they are to use one bookworm per week. Each day they are to read a passage from the Bible, a psalm, or a page from a Bible story book, then reward themselves with a piece of candy!

Pray:

When the bookworms are finished, invite kids to hold a candy bookworm and bow their heads. **Pray:** Dear God, We taste and see that you are good. Thank you for giving us your word to read. Amen.

Another Go:

Cut circles about two inches in diameter from a variety of colors of construction paper. Kids can staple or tape the circles together to create bookworm bookmarks for their Bibles.

THERE IS A SEASON

Bible Verse: "For everything there is a season, and a time for every matter under heaven." (Ecclesiastes 3:1)

Activity: Kids will enjoy seasonal food plates and think about the timeliness of certain activities and feelings.

Materials: Bible, paper, marker, four plates, aluminum foil, napkins, deviled eggs, salad greens, cherry tomatoes, cucumber and bell pepper slices, vegetable dip, grape clusters, apple slices, cookies or quick bread slices.

Ready:

Create four seasonal plates, washing, cooking, and preparing as needed: Spring—deviled eggs on greens; Summer—vegetables and dip; Autumn—fruit; Winter—baked goods. Cover each plate with aluminum foil to disguise contents until snack time.

Draw four symbols on a sheet of paper: a daffodil for spring; a blazing sun for summer; a falling leaf for autumn; and a snowflake for winter.

Set:

Keep the food plates aside. Place the symbol drawing on the table. As the kids come in, ask them to look at the drawing and think about what season each symbol represents.

Go!:

Hold up the symbol drawing and invite the kids to guess which season each symbol represents.

Next ask them to describe some particularly seasonal activities. After they respond, **say:** The world that God created has seasons and certain activities that go along with each season. For instance, we know that it is right to plant seeds in the spring, but it would be wacky to carve a pumpkin at Easter time. And the Bible tells us that there are times for other activities and feelings that aren't linked to any particular season.

Open the Bible and read Ecclesiastes 3:1-8. Read verse 3:1 again, then have the kids say it with you.

Ask: Can you think of a time you should weep? *(when you or a friend is hurt; when a scary thing happens)* A time when you should build something? *(after a tornado destroys a home; when kids need a new school)* A time to keep silent? *(when grownups are grumpy; when you're asked to keep a surprise)* A time to embrace or hug someone? *(when you are happy or sad for that person)*

Say: God understands that there is a time for each of our feelings and experiences.

Bring out the food plates and uncover them. Challenge the kids to guess which season is represented by each plate.

Pray:

Before the kids enjoy the snack, **pray:** Dear God, Thank you for the seasons and for a time for every matter under heaven. Amen.

Invite the kids to sample the treats from each season. Discuss the kids' favorite seasons and the moods or feelings that might be associated with each of them.

Another Go:

Bring out a roll of craft paper and paints and have the kids create a four seasons mural.

REJOICE!

Bible Verse: "This is a day that the Lord has made; let us rejoice and be glad in it." (Psalm 118:24)

Activity: Kids will rejoice with Sunshine Sundaes and a glad song.

Materials: Bible, hymnals, white posterboard or craft paper, marker, crayons, napkins, bowls, ice cream scoop, spoons, forks, pineapple rings, orange or lemon sherbert, tubes of yellow frosting

Ready:

The Sunshine Sundaes are made by laying a scoop of sherbert onto a chilled pineapple ring, then gilding it with yellow frosting sunrays. You'll need one 21-ounce can of pineapple for every ten kids.

Kid will learn the hymn "All Creatures of our God and King," found in most hymnals. You will need to have hymnals or song sheets available.

With a marker, draw a large sun with wavy or star point rays on the posterboard or craft paper. Locate lots of yellow and orange crayons.

Set:

Keep the pineapple and the sherbert in the refrigerator and freezer as long as possible before serving.

Place the sun drawing on a table along with the crayons. As the kids arrive, invite them to color the sun to make it shine!

Go!:

After the kids have colored the sun, **ask:** Where does the earth receive its natural light? *(the sun)* When day comes, where does the sun rise? *(in the east)* And where does the sun set? *(in the west)* Does the sun really move? *(No, the earth rotates around the sun, and the earth turns on its axis once in twenty-four hours.)* Who made the earth and the sun? *(God)*

Say: Even though the sun is ninety-three million miles from the earth, it is very important to our lives. The sun provides us with light, heat, and the beginning of each new day. Seeing the sun makes us feel glad!

Open the Bible and read the verse, then have the kids say it with you.

Next lead them in singing "All Creatures of our God and King." (With young children, perhaps just the first verse.) Tell the kids that St. Francis of Assisi wrote the words in 1255 in a poem called "Canticle to the Sun." St. Francis thought the sun was wonderful! Legend says that he wrote the poem on a hot, sunny summer day.

When the singing is finished, bring out the ingredients for the Sunshine sundaes, spoons, forks, and napkins. Let kids spear a pineapple ring and place it in the bottom of a bowl. Have them come to you for a big, round scoop of sherbert. Finally, they are to use the frosting to create beautiful rays of the sun.

Pray:

Before partaking of the sundaes, **pray:** Dear God, Thank you for this day. We rejoice and praise you for the song and the sundaes and the sun! Amen.

Have kids enjoy their sundaes before they melt.

As a final touch, write the verse on the sun that the kids colored and hang the poster in the classroom or the hall.

Another Go:

Purchase several paint pens and plastic sun visor hats, often available at dollar stores, and let the kids decorate them with suns and the word "Rejoice."

WORK TOGETHER FOR GOOD

Bible Verse: "We know that all things work together for good for those who love God." (Romans 8:28)

Activity: Working together, kids will assemble a pizza crust puzzle.

Materials: Bible, pizza dough, pizza sauce, cooking oil, baking sheet, rolling cutter or paring knife, several small bowls, napkins

Ready:

The pizza crust may be homemade or frozen. Prepare the crust ahead of time. Begin by preheating the oven to 425 degrees or as indicated on the package directions. Oil the baking sheet, then roll out or hand pat the dough to an even thickness on the sheet. Using the cutter or knife, create squiggly puzzle shaped lines in the uncooked dough. In this way, fashion enough puzzle pieces so that each child will have one.

Bake until crispy and golden brown, usually five minutes for thin crusts and ten minutes for thicker ones.

When the crust is done, remove it from the oven and cool. Gently break apart the puzzle pieces with fingers or a knife. After the pieces have been separated, allow them to cool, then place them in a bowl and cover.

Set:

Place the bowl of puzzle pieces and a baking sheet on the table where the kids will work. Have napkins and several small bowls with pizza sauce at hand.

Go!:

As kids arrive, have them wash their hands, then invite each of them to select a pizza piece from the bowl.

Ask: What do you think you are holding? *(a puzzle piece)* How is a puzzle assembled? *(by fitting all of the pieces together)* Is each of you needed to complete this puzzle? *(Yes, because we each have a piece.)*

Challenge the kids to work together on the puzzle. When they are finished, lead a round of applause.

Say: Life is like a puzzle, and many people, including us, hold pieces to the puzzle. Sometimes it is hard to understand what the puzzle looks like or where to fit the pieces in, but the Bible tells us that if we love God, all things will work together for good.

Open the Bible and read the verse, then have the kids say it with you.

Explain that just as you called upon the kids to piece the puzzle together, God will call upon each of them to help make all things work together for good.

Pray:

Have each child touch a pointed finger to his or her piece of the puzzle.

Pray: Dear God, We know that you love us. We will remember that all things work together for good if we also love you. Amen.

Direct the kids to pick up their pieces, wave them over their heads, and say the verse. Bring out the bowls of sauce and napkins, then invite the kids to break apart their crusts and dip them into the sauce for a snack.

Another Go:

On a piece of posterboard, let kids write the verse and decorate around it with a marker. Cut the posterboard apart into puzzle pieces and invite another group at church to work the puzzle.

Mighty Minds

THINGS VISIBLE AND INVISIBLE

Bible Verse: "For in him all things in heaven and on earth were created, things visible and invisible." (Colossians 1:16)

Activity: As they pretend to remove gifts from the Invisible Present Box, kids will think about the visible and the invisible.

Materials: Bible, box, small gifts (optional)

Ready:

Find a pretty box or decorate one to be the Invisible Present Box. The box needs to be large enough so that kids can put their hands in it to pull out invisible presents.

At the end of the activity you may want to give each of the kids a small visible present too such as a bookmark, pencil, or candy.

Set:

As kids arrive, address them by name and **say:** I am so glad I can see you today!

Go!

Gather the kids together and begin. **Say:** I'm going to point to each of you one at a time and ask you to tell me something that you have seen today that you really like. After the kids respond, **say:** It's great that God has given us a world with so many wonderful things to see. Now I'm going to ask you to do something that is more difficult. I'm going to point to each of you, and I want you to tell me something about the world that you really like that is invisible and that you cannot see. If kids need help, name some invisible wonders yourself such as God, love, faith, happiness, courage, and loyalty.

Say: There is a verse in the Bible that talks about the visible and the invisible.

Open the Bible and read the verse, then have the kids say it with you.

Continue: In honor of the idea of invisible wonders and gifts, I have some invisible presents for you in my Invisible Present Box. I would like to give one to each of you.

Invite the kids to come forward, one at a time, to choose an invisible present. As they choose, you can add to the intrigue by making comments such as "Oh you've made an excellent choice" and "What a lovely invisible present."

Remind them to hold their presents carefully and not to forget them when they leave!

Consider having kids tell the group what invisible presents they chose, although they may enjoy keeping them a secret.

Pray:

Ask kids to continue holding their invisible presents during the prayer.

Pray: Dear God, All things were created by you and through your son, Jesus; all things visible and invisible. Thank you! Amen.

Give the kids the small visible presents, too, if you have them.

Another Go:

Consider inviting an invisible friend to join you for this activity or an upcoming one. Kids can have fun naming the friend, introducing themselves, and telling the friend about their church.

THE LORD LOOKS AT THE HEART

Bible Verse: "The Lord does not see as mortals see; they look on the outward appearance, but the Lord looks at the heart." (1 Samuel 16:7)

Activity: Kids will record one of their heart's desires on a paper heart.

Materials: Bible, pennies, red paper, scissors, pens or markers

Ready:

Kids will cut paper into heart shapes. You may want to do this ahead of time for younger kids.

Set:

As kids arrive, hand them a penny and **say:** A penny for your thoughts!

Go!:

When all have arrived, call the kids together and begin. **Say:** I gave you a penny this morning and said, "A penny for your thoughts." That's an old-fashioned expression. What it means is: Another person can't read your thoughts, and so for fun, they offer you a penny to tell what you are thinking. But God knows your thoughts. God can see into our hearts and our minds. Listen to this verse.

Open the Bible and read the verse, then have the kids say it with you. (Explain that "mortals" is another word for human beings.)

Say: This verse helps us to realize that God understands us. There is another old-fashioned expression, "Your heart's desire." Your heart's desire is something that you really want. God knows your heart's desire. God knows what it is that you really want.

Explain to the kids that their heart's desires need not be material things. Have them consider non-material things such as a sport they wish they could play well, a hobby they would like to take up, a skill they hope to develop, or a friendship they want to make stronger.

Give each child a piece of red paper. Demonstrate how to fold the paper in half and cut a heart. Next, ask kids to write one of their heart's desires on the paper heart without showing anyone else. When this is finished, have them hold their paper hearts over their real hearts with the writing facing inward. Choose a child and have everyone try to guess what his or her heart's desire is. Then have the child show the paper heart to the group. Continue until everyone has had a turn.

Say: It's fun to offer a penny for someone's thoughts or to share a heart's desire, but it's most important to remember that God knows what's in our hearts before we even speak. And so when we approach God in prayer, we can speak openly and honestly.

Pray:

Have kids hold their paper hearts against their real hearts one more time. Ask them to close their eyes as you **pray:** Dear God, We know that you do not see as people see. People look on the outward appearance, but you look at our hearts. May the thoughts of our minds and the desires of our hearts be acceptable to you. Amen.

Another Go:

Have kids make paper plate masks with faces very different from their own. While they are wearing their masks, ask them questions that call for feelings and opinions. Point out that while their outward appearance has changed, they haven't changed on the inside at all.

THE BEGINNING AND THE END

Bible Verse: "I am the Alpha and the Omega, the first and the last, the beginning and the end." (Revelation 22:13)

Activity: Reading the beginning and the ending of a picture book about Jesus will help kids think about the meaning of this verse.

Materials: Bible, picture book, alphabet cereal, cups

Ready:

Check your home, church, or public library for a picture book about Jesus such as *Good News Travels Fast: An Easter Story* by Lisa Flinn and Barbara Younger (Abingdon Press, 2001).

Set:

Pour cereal into the cups and have them waiting as kids arrive. As you hand them the cereal, **say:** An A to Z snack for you today.

Go!:

After kids have enjoyed the snack, **ask:** What were you just eating? *(alphabet cereal)* **Say:** I gave you letters of the alphabet to introduce you to today's Bible verse.

Open the Bible and read the verse, then have the kids say it with you.

Continue: The Alpha and the Omega are the first and last letters of the Greek Alphabet, one of the alphabets of Jesus' day. And the first and last letters of our alphabet are A and Z. **Ask:** Why do you think the alphabet is important? *(Because without it, we would not be able to read.)* **Say:** Thanks to our alphabet, we can read books such as this one about Jesus (hold up the book).

Next, hand the book to someone and **say:** Please read us the first two sentences of this book. Then hand the book to another child and **say:** Will you please read us the last two sentences of the book. (You can do this if your kids don't read.)

Close the book and **say:** Now we've read the beginning and the ending of a story about Jesus. Jesus compared himself to the Alpha and the Omega, the beginning and the end, the first and the last, to help us understand that he is the most important part of our lives.

Next hold up the book and **ask:** Is this really the right way to read a book? *(No)* **Say:** In the Bible verse, Jesus points out how important he is to all of us by saying that he is the beginning and the end. The beginning and the ending do always seem to be the most important parts of a story. But Jesus is the middle too! Jesus is the whole story.

Read the picture book to the kids. Take a few minutes to discuss the book and what it says about Jesus and his importance to our lives.

Pray:

Explain to the kids that they will say the beginning of the prayer with you by reciting the alphabet, then you will finish the prayer. **Pray:** (Say the alphabet) Dear God, Thank you for Jesus, our Teacher and our Savior from A to Z. Amen.

Another Go:

Give kids Bibles and have them look up and read the first and the last verses of both the Old and the New Testaments.

YOU SHALL LOVE YOUR NEIGHBOR

Bible Verse: "You shall love your neighbor as yourself." (Matthew 22:39)

Activity: Kids will think about the importance of loving their neighbors, then make puzzles to share with them.

Materials: Bible, puzzles, magazines, construction paper, glue, scissors, reclosable food storage bags

Ready:

To make the puzzles, kids will look through magazines to find a picture they think their neighbor will like. They will then glue the picture to a piece of construction paper and cut it apart into a puzzle.

Just for fun, kids will work on one or several puzzles when they arrive. If your church has puzzles with religious themes, use them for this activity. If not, bring in puzzles from home. Puzzles should be simple enough so that kids can complete them before and at the close of the activity.

Set:

Have the puzzles set up. As kids arrive, invite them to work on them.

Go!

Even if the kids haven't finished the puzzles, call them together when it's time to begin, explaining that they may finish the puzzles at the end of the activity.

Begin by asking kids to each say the name of one of their neighbors and to tell a tiny bit about that person. **Say:** Sometimes we are friendly with our neighbors and sometimes we might have trouble getting along with them. But God wants us to love our neighbors. This is one of the most important commandments that Jesus gave us.

Open the Bible and read the verse, then have the kids say it with you.

Ask: Is it always easy to love your neighbor? After the kids respond, **say:** Sometimes our neighbors are fun and it's easy to love them, but sometimes we may have neighbors who are unfriendly and it's harder to show our love to them. But this is what Jesus wants us to do.

Explain to the kids that they can show love to their neighbors by spending time with them. **Say:** Jesus says that we are to love our neighbors as we love ourselves. One of the ways you can do this is by sharing an activity with your neighbor that you enjoy, such as working puzzles. Remind kids that they should never visit a neighbor without first getting permission from their parents.

Tell kids that now they will make their own puzzles to share with their neighbors. Encourage them to look through the magazines for pictures they think their neighbors will appreciate. Once the pictures are glued onto the construction paper, kids should cut the picture into a puzzle. Younger children can simply cut their picture into four squares. Older kids may want to cut more complicated shapes. Warn them that cutting the puzzle into more than eight to ten pieces can render it too difficult to piece back together.

When the puzzles are finished, have the kids put them into the reclosable bags. Suggest that in the next week or so, they find a time when they can get together with their neighbor to put the puzzle together, reminding them once again, not to do this without the permission of their parents.

Pray:

Ask kids to link elbows or join hands as you **pray:** Dear God, Help us to remember the commandment of Jesus: Love your neighbor as yourself. Make us good neighbors. Amen.

Another Go:

Many kids are aware of folks in their community who are sick, grieving, or elderly. Make a Prayer Neighborhood for your room. On a piece of posterboard, have the kids each draw a house. Then on the house, ask them to write the name of a neighbor they would like to include in a prayer you say together.

A LAMP TO MY FEET

Bible Verse: "Your word is a lamp to my feet and a light to my path." (Psalm 119:105))

Activity: Kids will use a flashlight to read the verse from the Word of God Box, then look through their Bibles to find other words of God.

Materials: Bibles, shoebox, marker, paper, tape, pencils or pens, scissors, flashlight

Ready:

To create the Word of God Box you will need a shoebox or other box with a lid. Write the Bible verse on a piece of paper cut to fit the inside end of the box. Tape the verse inside one end. Cut about a 4-inch square down from the top of the other end, then put the lid back on the box. Kids will use a flashlight to peer through the hole and read the verse.

For the second part of the activity, kids will look through the Bible to find words that they find meaningful. Even beginning readers will be able to recognize some words they know. You may want to write words such as "Jesus," "Lord," and "God" on the classroom board and direct them to the easiest places in the Bible to find those words. Kids will write the words they find on slips of paper and drop them into the Word of God Box.

Set:

As kids arrive, hand them the flashlight and invite them to look into the Word of God Box. Once they are looking into the box, ask them to read what they see. Even kids who don't read yet will enjoy using the flashlight to see the verse. Once they see it, you can say it for them.

Go!:

After everyone has had a turn to look into the box, ask if someone can say the verse. If this isn't successful, ask if someone can remember any of the words from the verse and/or what the verse is about. Then invite a child to take a turn with the flashlight again and read the verse for the group. Finally, have the kids say the verse with you.

Ask: What does it mean that God's word is a lamp to our feet and a light to our path? (*The Bible is our guide for living the life God wants us to live.*)

Say: Just as lamps and lights help us to see and walk at night, God's word helps Christians understand how God wants us to live.

Give a Bible to each child, and have the paper and pencils ready. **Say:** The Bible is the word of God and it is filled with words that express our faith. Look through the Bible and write down some of the words that you recognize that speak to you of our Christian faith.

After kids write down a word, invite them to drop it into the Word of God Box.

Pray:

When each child has put a few words into the box, ask them to close their Bibles, reminding them that they can read the Word of God at home, too. Next explain that you will use some of their words in the prayer. **Pray:** Dear God, We thank you for the Bible, your word to us, and for the wonderful words of our faith. Here are some of the words we found today. (Read some or all of the words.) "Your word is a lamp to our feet and a light to our path." (Psalm 119:105) Amen.

Another Go:

Teach kids the old time favorite, "The B-I-B-L-E." Here are the lyrics: The B-I-B-L-E, yes that's the book for me, I stand alone on the Word of God, The B-I-B-L-E. You may want to have the kids make large flashcards of each letter to hold up while they sing.

HEAR MY CHILD

Bible Verse: "Hear, my child, your father's instruction, and do not reject you mother's teaching." (Proverbs 1:8)

Activity: Kids will create Good Advice Plaques to present to their parents.

Materials: Bible, lined writing paper, construction paper, pencils or pens, stapler, markers or crayons.

Ready:

To make the Good Advice Plaques, kids will write down a piece of advice their parents have given them on a sheet of lined writing paper. Lined paper often comes in tablets that measure about 6 by 9 inches. The paper will then be stapled to a piece of light colored construction paper. Kids will decorate the borders of the construction paper with simple drawings that reflect their parents' advice.

Set

As kids arrive, greet them by using a piece of advice your parents gave you. You might say, as you shake hands, "Good morning, my father always said it was important to give a firm handshake." Encourage the kids to share some of the advice their parents have given them. **Then say:** Parents certainly do like to give advice! There is a verse in the Bible that tells us to listen to this advice.

Go!

Parents give advice because that's their job, and because they love their children. And the Bible backs them up. Tell the kids that they are going to make Good Advice Plaques to give to their parents to thank them for their good advice. Give them each a piece of the lined paper and a pencil or a pen. Ask them to think for a few minutes about an important piece of advice their parents have given them, then have them write the advice on the paper. Assist younger kids with writing.

Next, have the kids staple the paper to a piece of construction paper. Finally, they are to decorate the borders of the construction paper with symbols that reflect the advice. For example, they might draw stop signs and/or cars if they are told to watch crossing the street; vegetables if they are instructed to eat plenty of them; books if they are encouraged to read; or smiley faces if they are admonished to be more cheerful.

Pray:

Ask kids to hold their Good Advice Plaques while you **pray:** Dear God, Today we learned this Bible verse: "Hear, my child, your father's instruction, and do not reject you mother's teaching." (Proverbs 1:8) Help us to happily take the good advice of our parents. Amen.

Tell kids that they are to present the Good Advice Plaques to their parents when they next see them.

Another Go:

You may have some older members of your congregation who would love to visit with your kids and share some of their own bits of wisdom.

YOU ARE GOD'S TEMPLE

Bible Verse: "Do you not know that you are God's temple and that God's spirit dwells in you?" (1 Corinthians 3:16)

Activity: Kids will each make a Paper Me to help them think about taking care of their own bodies.

Materials: Bible, 8 1/2 by 11 inch paper, paper fasteners, scissors, markers or crayons

Ready:

Make a sample Paper Me. Cut an oval body out of one piece of paper, simple arms and legs out of another, and a head out of a third. Put the body together using the paper fasteners. Decorate the Paper Me to look like you, with hair and features (but skip the clothes!)

Set:

As kids arrive, let your Paper Me do a bit of dancing and say: I just love to exercise!

Go!:

Gather the kids together and invite them to sit down. **Say:** And now I'm going to ask you to stand up! We're going to begin today with a bit of exercise for our bodies. Lead the kids in some energetic jumping jacks or jogging in place, then invite them to sit down again.

Say: Exercise is good for our bodies. **Ask:** What else is good for our bodies? *(rest, water, proper nutrition, sleep, practicing safety such as wearing seat belts and bike helmets)* **Continue:** Our bodies are gifts to us from God, and God wants us to take care of them. There is a Bible verse that calls our body "God's temple." Listen.

Open the Bible and read the verse, then have the kids say it with you.

Say: A temple is a sacred place. The Bible verse is saying that our bodies are sacred places too, just like temples. The spirit of God lives in our bodies and so we need to take especially good care of them.

Tell the kids that they are each going to make their own Paper Me. Guide them as they cut out the parts of the body, fasten them together, and add hair and features.

Pray:

Ask kids to look into the eyes of their Paper Me as they repeat after you: *I promise to take care of me each and every day!* Then ask them to hug their Paper Me as you **pray:** Dear God, I know that I am your temple and that your spirit dwells within me. Help me to take good care of my body. Amen.

Tell kids to give their Paper Me an honored place in their rooms at home.

Another Go:

Invite a health care provider in your congregation to come and talk to the kids, perhaps bringing along some of the more interesting instruments he or she uses at work such as a stethoscope or a blood pressure cuff.

GIVE THANKS IN ALL CIRCUMSTANCES

Bible Verse: "Give thanks in all circumstances; for this is the will of God in Christ Jesus for you." (1 Thessalonians 5:18)

Activity: After hearing the story of the first chocolate chip cookie, kids will think about thanking God and finding good in every situation.

Materials: Bible, chocolate chip cookies, plate

Ready:

Bake or purchase chocolate chip cookies

Set:

Put the cookies on a plate. As kids arrive, offer them a cookie.

Say: In a few minutes, I'm going to tell you how the chocolate chip cookie was invented.

Go!:

After the kids have enjoyed their cookie, begin. **Say:** Chocolate chip cookies are delicious, but I bet you didn't know that they were invented as the result of something that went wrong. In the 1930's, Ruth Wakefield was baking chocolate

cookies for the guests at her inn in Whitman, Massachusetts. She ran out of baker's chocolate, so she broke up a semi-sweet chocolate bar and put it into her cookie batter. She thought the pieces would melt to make chocolate cookies. But the pieces of chocolate did not melt, and the first chocolate chip cookies were created quite by accident.

Continue: Mrs. Whitman's cookies are an example of a good thing that came about as a result of something bad. She ran out of the chocolate she needed, which was annoying, and the chocolate she substituted did not melt, which was a disappointment. But she ended up inventing something really delicious!

Ask: Have any of you ever had a mistake or an accident or a bad situation turn into something good? (Share an experience or two of your own.) **Then say:** Many times good things come out of bad circumstances. Those good things aren't always something as visible as cookies. Sometimes, we learn patience or understanding from a bad situation or we become stronger or wiser.

Open the Bible and read the verse, then have the kids say it with you.

Say: This verse tells us to give thanks to God in all circumstances. "All circumstances" means in every single situation that we encounter. The next time something bad happens, try thanking God and asking God to help you make good things come from that situation.

Pray:

Ask the kids to close their eyes and bow their heads as you **pray:** Dear God, We're glad that Mrs. Whitman's chocolate didn't melt so that she could invent the first chocolate chip cookie. We thank you for good things that come from bad situations. May we learn to give thanks in all circumstances. Amen.

Another Go:

Make a list of difficult situations and let kids brainstorm good that could come from them. Situations might include: a case of the flu, a bad report card, a broken CD player, a rained-out field day, a lost wallet, a missing pet, an angry parent, a friend who moves away, and a melted ice cream sandwich.

Busy Hands

COVERS THE HEAVENS WITH CLOUDS

Bible Verse: "He covers the heavens with clouds, prepares rain for the earth, makes grass grow on the hills." (Psalm 147:8)

Activity: After mixing their own shaving foam paint, kids will create a painting reflecting the psalm's imagery.

Materials: Bible, spray bottle, one container of unscented white shaving foam, green and blue food coloring, 3 ounce bathroom cups, drinking straws or beverage stirrers, spoons, white paper plates, pen, a recording of rainfall or other nature sounds and a player (optional)

Ready:

Each child will need two bathroom cups to hold the shaving foam, a straw or stirrer to mix the coloring into the foam, a spoon for painting, and a paper plate for a canvas.

Set:

Fill the spray bottle with water. When each child arrives, invite him or her to spray a mist into the air and walk under it. Monitor this activity so that kids do not spray each other.

Go!:

When everyone has experienced the spray, **ask:** When you sprayed the water and felt it falling on you, what did it remind you of? *(rain, fog, playing in the sprinkler, the shower)* Can you think of a time when you were caught in a sudden shower? After the kids respond, **ask:** Where does the rain fall from? *(clouds)* Why do we need rain? *(for plants to grow and people and animals to live)*

Say: There is a verse in the Bible that speaks of the rain and clouds that God created.

Open the Bible and read the verse, then have the kids say it with you.

Say: This verse is from the book of Psalms. The songs and poetry of the Psalms are some of the most descriptive and beautiful writings in the Bible. Hearing or reading a psalm can bring forth a picture in our minds.

Tell kids to close their eyes and picture the verse as you read it again.

Then say: And now, you are going to paint a real picture of the verse.

Give each child two cups. Squirt enough shaving foam in each cup to cover the bottom of the cup. The foam will quickly expand. First go around the group and put three drops of green food coloring in one of the cups. Then go back around again and put three drops of blue food coloring in the rest of the cups. Direct the kids to mix the coloring into their cups with the straws or stirrers. With stirring, the foam will expand even more.

As kids mix their paints, label a paper plate for each child with his or her name. Invite kids to use the rounded edge of a spoon to apply the paint to their paper plate canvases. As they do, encourage them to create a painting that reflects the verse. If you have a recording of rain or other nature sounds, play it as the group paints.

When the artists are finished, compliment their work, **then say:** Just as a cloudy, rainy sky can change, so will these puffy pictures change as they dry. They will stay just as colorful, but the paint will flatten. It takes a whole day for the foam to evaporate and dry.

If possible, hand the foamy canvases over to parents to carefully transport home. If not, urge kids to carry them home with care. They will be interested to watch their paintings change.

Pray:

Gather the group and look out of the windows skyward as you **pray:** Dear God, We thank you for the blessings of clouds and rain and green grass and the fun of painting. Amen.

Another Go:

Share a few more psalms and some haiku or other nature poetry with your kids, then have them write their own poems about God's natural world.

DO NOT LET YOUR HEARTS BE TROUBLED

Bible Verse: "Do not let your hearts be troubled, and do not let them be afraid." (John 14:27b)

Activity: Kids will craft Prayer Pillows decorated with the verse to comfort them when they feel worried.

Materials: Bible, muslin, cloth ribbon, polyester fiberfill, a roll of fusible hem tape, ruler, pencil, crayons, scissors, iron, dishtowel, paper towels, watch with a second hand, candy conversation hearts or small paper hearts

Ready:

Purchase muslin that is 36 inches from selvage to selvage, so that the ends of the pillow will have finished edges. For each pillow, you'll need one-half yard of muslin, one yard of ribbon, and one yard of fusible hem tape. One twenty ounce bag of polyester fiberfill will stuff 6 pillows.

Wash and dry fabric and cut into 18-inch lengths, selvage to selvage. Cut the ribbon in 18 inch lengths and the fusible hem tape into 36 inch lengths.

On the muslin, measure in 6 inches from each selvage and make several marks with a pencil. This will form the outside boundary for coloring and will show where to tie the ribbons.

Finally, if you cannot find candy conversation hearts, cut small hearts from paper and write phrases such as "You're great," "Be kind," or "I like you" on each heart.

Set:

Establish your ironing station away from the path of the kids. Lay out the dishtowel as a pad and set out the iron, paper towels, fusible tape, and watch. Always use caution when operating an iron around children, and do not let them touch the iron. Place the muslin pieces and crayons around the table. As kids come in, offer them a candy or a paper heart.

Go:

When everyone has arrived, **say:** These hearts all have fun, sweet messages on them, which make our real hearts feel happy. But sometimes our hearts can feel unhappy and troubled.

Ask: Can you think of some reasons you might feel troubled? *(a run-in with a bully, a sick parent, a mean teacher, a fear of storms)*

Say: We all have times when we feel troubled. Listen to what Jesus told his disciples.

Open the Bible and read the verse, then have the kids say it with you.

Continue: Jesus spoke these words to his disciples before his death because he did not want them to be worried and afraid. Jesus does not want us to be worried, either. Instead, he wants us to talk to him in prayer. To help you remember this, we're going to make Prayer Pillows.

Write: "Do not let your hearts be troubled" on the classroom board or a piece of paper for kids to copy. Explain that they are to write these words with crayons on the fabric. Show the pencil margin marks and encourage them to write with bold, thick strokes of crayon. Younger kids may need assistance.

As kids finish, turn the iron on to the "cotton" setting. One at a time, place each piece of fabric colored side up. Put a paper towel over the colored letters, and press with the hot iron for 30 seconds over the whole surface. The heat sets the color permanently into the fabric.

Press all of the colored pieces first, then work on seaming the pillowcases together. Overlap the 36-inch scissor cut edges by one-half inch. Between the overlap, place the 36-inch length of fusible tape. Press the hot iron over one section of the overlap at a time for 15 seconds. Do not move the iron around. Repeat until the seam is fused.

Have kids tie the ribbon over the pencil marks at one end, then stuff fiberfill into the pillow casing. Seal by tying another ribbon on the pencil marks at the other end.

Pray:

Invite kids to hug their new Prayer Pillows as you **pray:** Dear God, We know that when our hearts our troubled, we can pray to you and to your son, Jesus. Amen.

Another Go:

Crayon release drawings are fun! Purchase white T-shirts or handkerchiefs. Wash, dry, and have kids decorate using the method above.

God So Loved The World

Bible Verse: "For God so loved the world that he gave his only Son, so that everyone who believes in him may not perish, but may have eternal life." (John 3:16)

Activity: Using a map and index cards, kids will create Good News Postcards.

Materials: Bible, one old or new folded paper map, 4 by 6-inch index cards, glue sticks or glue, markers, rulers, scissors, postcard stamps

Ready:

If your old map is crumpled, it can be pressed out with a medium hot iron. If a new map is in order, most drug and general stores, as well as gas stations, carry city and state maps. Plan for kids to make several postcards each by gluing a piece of the map to one side of an index card and placing a stamp and an address on the other side.

Set:

As kids arrive, invite them to study the map, identifying countries, states, cities, bodies of water, or special features such as bike paths and topographical information. Discuss the key to the map. Let kids use a ruler to measure distances between points.

Go!:

When kids have enjoyed a thorough inspection of the map, **say:** Looking at this map reminds us that the world is a big place that is filled with many people.

Ask: Who created the world and all that is in it, including the people? *(God)* Do you think that God loves the world and its people? *(Yes)*

Say: The Gospel of John speaks of God's love.

Open the Bible and read the verse, then have the kids say it with you.

Ask: What does it mean that God "gave his only Son?" *(God sent Jesus to live among us and teach us, then to die as our savior on the cross for the forgiveness of our sins.)* If we believe in Jesus, will we have eternal life? *(Yes)*

Say: This verse is one of the most well-known and beloved verses in the Bible. It has a message of good news: God loves us and through our faith in Jesus, we will have life after death.

Explain that now the group will make Good News Postcards. Begin by laying a row of index cards end to end across one edge of the map. Use the cards as a

guide to mark a strip. Cut the strip and use it to mark and cut out more strips. Have kids place their index cards on the map strips to mark and cut a piece that will completely cover one side of the card.

Ask them to glue the map piece to the card, then write "John 3:16" on the piece of map. On the flip side of each card, have them put a stamp in the right hand corner. In the center of the cards, kids should put the name of someone to whom they would like to send the card. They can find the addresses at home with the help of their parents. Suggest that each child make at least one card to send to church members who may be lonely or ill. Use the church directory to locate those addresses.

When the Good News Postcards are completed, ask kids to gather round to sing "He's Got the Whole World In His Hands."

Pray:

Have kids hold hands in a circle. **Pray:** Dear God, Thank you for loving the world, for giving us your only Son, and for eternal life. Amen.

Another Go:

Have access to a button pin machine? Cover the face of the buttons with pieces of map and write "John 3:16" with a dark marker. Let the kids give the pins to fellow church members. Don't have a button machine? Use adhesive package labels.

WE ARE THE CLAY

Bible Verse: "We are the clay, and you are our potter; we are all the work of your hand." (Isaiah 64:8)

Activity: Kids will use modeling dough to mold people, pots, and something they especially love from God's creation.

Materials: Bible, modeling dough, wax paper, reclosable food storag bags

Ready:

Purchase modeling dough or make your own from the following recipe. Homemade dough tends to crumble less than commercial dough.

To make modeling dough: Mix two cups flour with one cup salt and four tea-spoons cream of tartar. Add several drops food coloring and two tablespoons of cooking oil to two cups of water. Stir into dry ingredients and cook over medium heat until mixture begins to form a ball. Cool and knead. Store in an air-tight container until ready to use. This recipe yields enough modeling dough for ten kids.

Set:

Tear wax paper into squares and put about 1/3 cup of dough onto each square, one per child. Place the squares around the table.

Go!:

Gather the kids around the table. Ask them not to touch the dough just yet.

Ask: What does a potter do? *(molds pots and other articles out of clay)* **Say:** There is a verse in the book of Isaiah that compares God to a potter.

Open the Bible and read the verse, then have the kids say it with you.

Ask: How is God like a potter? *(Because God created and molded us.)*

Invite kids to mold their dough into the shape of a person. As they work, have them say several times, "We are the clay." When they are finished, ask them to show the people they have created to the group, one at a time.

Next, have kids mold their dough into the shape of a pot. As they work, have them say several times, "You are our potter." When they are finished, ask them to show their pots to one another.

Finally, have kids mold their dough into something that they especially love in God's creation *(animals, plants, natural formations such as caves or volcanoes)*. As they work, have them say several times, "We are all the work of your hand." When the creations are finished have them show what they have molded and tell why they especially love that creation. Give kids the reclosable bags so they may package their dough and take them home.

Pray:

Ask kids to fold their hands. **Pray:** Dear God, We thank you for making us and for making all of the wonders of your creation. We are the clay, and you are our potter. We are all the work of your hands. Amen.

Another Go:

This verse may be sung to the tune of "His Banner Over Me is Love."

WHERE YOUR TREASURE IS

Bible Verse: "For where your treasure is, there your heart will be also." (Matthew 6:21)

Activity: While on a treasure hunt, kids will discover unusual booty and learn that their real treasure is their faith.

Materials: Bible, paper, marker, aluminum foil, Christian button pins or lapel pins, mixing bowl, fork, measuring cup, baking sheet, potholder, 1 1/2 cup flour, 1 1/2 cup coffee grounds, 1 cup salt, 1/2 cup sand or cornmeal, 1 cup water

Ready:

The recipe for Rocky Treasures makes enough for eight kids. The recipe may be doubled.

Purchase inexpensive buttons or pins that reflect the Christian faith. Wrap each in a bit of aluminum foil.

Make Rocky Treasures by mixing the dry ingredients in a bowl. With a fork, slowly stir in the water until the mixture resembles a stiff cookie dough. Make eight balls about the size of an extra large egg. With your thumb, press a hole in each ball. Place the foil-wrapped treasure in the hole, then mold and compress the dough around the hole until the contents are covered. Put the Rocky Treasures on a baking sheet and slide them into a 200 degree oven for twenty minutes. Remove and allow to cool at least one-half hour before use. Rocky Treasures may also be air dried for several days.

Using paper and the marker, draw a treasure map that will lead the kids from the room to the treasure spot. To add to the fun, draw landmarks on your map and indicate how many paces the kids will step.

When the treasure rocks are opened they can make a few crumbs. If indoors, you may want to have kids open them over newspaper or paper towels.

Set:

Place the Rocky Treasures in the treasure spot.

As the kids arrive, invite them to study the treasure map.

Go!:

After all have arrived, begin the hunt with the rule that the group must stay together. When the kids reach the treasure, they may not realize that the inconspicuous-looking lumps are what they are looking for.

Ask: What do you expect to find on a treasure hunt? *(treasure)* What did you see instead? *(funny looking rocks)* Why don't you find out what's inside! After the kids open the Rocky Treasures, **say:** Sometimes, treasure is not what we expect it to be. Listen to what Jesus says about treasure.

Open the Bible and read Matthew 6:19-21, then have the kids say verse 21 with you.

Say: The Bible tells us that the only lasting treasures we have are love and faith. The good things we do for others through love are the treasures we can store up in heaven. Our faith in Jesus is what will bring us to heaven someday.

Say a word to the kids about the symbols or words of their brand new buttons or pins. After they pin the buttons over their hearts, have the kids say the verse again with you.

Pray:

Have kids hold their hands over their hearts as you **pray:** Dear God, We will remember that real treasures are stored in heaven and that's where our hearts will be also. Amen.

Another Go:

Have kids mix up a batch or two of the Rocky Treasures dough and put wrapped candy or trinkets inside the rocks. Let your kids enjoy hosting a treasure hunt for another group.

FRIENDS

Bible Verse: "You are my friends." (John 15:14, adapted)

Activity: Making Faith Friend button dolls will remind kids that within the church they have many friends.

Materials: Bible, buttons, beads, pipe cleaners, fine tip permanent markers, scissors

Ready:

Purchase buttons and pipe cleaners in a variety of colors, if possible. For each doll you will need: Body: eight 1/2-inch buttons; Hat: one 1-inch button (girls) or one 1/2-inch or smaller button (boys); Head: one 1/2inch to 1 1/2-inch bead or same size button with a shank end (with one loop on back); Arms: one 2-inch length of pipe cleaner, Body and Legs: one 6-inch length of pipe cleaner.

Make a sample doll according to the directions that follow in "Go."

Invite a few church members to visit with your group and assist with the project. Try to find people of both genders and several age groups.

Please note that the small parts of these button dolls may present a choking hazard and should not be given to young children.

Set:

As the kids arrive, ask your visitors to greet them by introducing themselves, shaking hands, and using the phrase "faith friend." For example, "Hi, my name is Kisha, and I'm one of your faith friends" or "Nice to see you, Charlie. I'm Peg. I'm glad you're my faith friend."

Go:!

Gather everyone around the table and **say:** I know you have friends at school or work, in the neighborhood, and with your clubs. It's great to have many friends in many places.

Ask: What's good about having friends at school? *(someone to eat lunch with; study with; talk to)* What's good about having friends in your neighborhood? *(someone to play with and visit)* What's good about having friends in your clubs? *(someone to share your interests)* Now, can you tell me what's special about having friends at church? *(We share a faith in Jesus.)*

Say: Jesus wants us to love one another as he loves us. He called his disciples "friends", and he wants us to be friends with one another, too.

Open the Bible and read the verse, then have the kids say it with you.

Begin the craft by asking everyone to pick up a 6-inch length of pipe cleaner and bend it in half, so that both stems are side by side. Thread both stems into the holes of the hat button, then push both stems through the center hole of the bead or button head. Slide the head up to the hat.

Next, thread the eight 1/2-inch buttons onto the pipe cleaner stems, one by one, pushing each toward the head. This forms the body. Now bend the 2-inch pipe cleaner length in half and slide it between the first and second buttons. Twist once around the pipe cleaner body, then open the ends to make the arms. Push the buttons of the body gently upward, then twist the pipe cleaner legs twice to hold the buttons in place.

Use the marker to make eyes and a smile. The Faith Friend is finished!

Pray:

Ask the group to hold their Faith Friend dolls and link arms with their real faith friends. **Pray:** Dear God, We are grateful for all of our faith friends and deeply thankful for Jesus, who brings us together. Amen.

Another Go:

Have a Faith Friends Fiesta with refreshments such as cake, chips, fruit, and punch. Invite more friends from church to come to the party and spend time getting to know one another better.

THE CROSS OF OUR LORD

Bible Verse: "May I never boast of anything except the cross of our Lord Jesus Christ." (Galatians 6:14a)

Activity: Boasting only of their belief in Jesus, kids will paint and draw chalk crosses on the sidewalk.

Materials: Bible, sidewalk chalk, spray bottles, cornstarch, a four-color box of food coloring, water, measuring cup with spout or mixing bowl and funnel, measuring spoons, spoon.

Ready:

Purchase thick sticks of sidewalk chalk and the ingredients for the chalk paint. Locate four spray bottles *(one for each color)* with adjustable nozzles that allow the contents to be squirted in a stream. If you're short on bottles, you can mix fewer colors.

If you have a measuring cup with a pour spout, use it for mixing the paint, otherwise, use a small mixing bowl and a funnel to pour the paint into the bottles.

To mix the chalk paint, follow these steps with each color:

First, measure (6 ounces) of water into cup or bowl. To this, add 9 tablespoons of cornstarch. Stir with a spoon, mashing any lumps with the rounded back of the spoon. When the mixture is smooth, drop in 25-30 drops of one color of food coloring and stir. Pour into a spray bottle. Repeat with the remaining colors.

Unfortunately, if the weather doesn't cooperate, you will need to save this activity for another day!

Set:

As kids arrive, greet each person with a boast such as "Hi Bonita, did you know that I bake the world's most delicious cookies?" or "Hello, Ty. I want to tell you that I am the best dog trainer there ever was."

Go!:

When everyone has arrived, begin by **asking**: Was I just doing a lot of bragging and boasting? *(Yes!)* What does it mean to "boast?" *(to talk about yourself too proudly)* How do you feel when other people boast to you about themselves? *(irritated, bored, angry)*

Say: Even in Bible times, boasting was a bit of a problem. Listen to what Paul says to the Galatians about boasting.

Open the Bible and read the verse, then have the kids say it with you.

Continue: Paul is saying that there is nothing that he, or anyone else, should boast about except our belief in Jesus and our salvation on the cross. For today's activity, we're going to show our pride in Jesus by painting and drawing crosses on the sidewalk. Those who walk by will see how proud we are to be Christians.

Explain that the kids will take turns using the chalk spray paint and the chalk sticks when outside. When outside, demonstrate how to spray a cross (one squirt down and one squirt across), then hand out the chalk supplies. Caution against spraying one another, since the paint contains dye that may stain. Also note that the paint should not be used on vertical surfaces such as steps or walls, because it drips and runs.

Pray:

Gather the kids around the beautifully decorated sidewalk and repeat the verse with them, then **pray:** Dear God, May we never boast of anything except our belief in the cross of Jesus. Amen.

It's nice to leave the crosses for others to admire, but if necessary, the chalk may be swept away with a broom or rinsed away with water.

Another Go:

Black construction paper makes a perfect background for the lovely pastel shades of chalk. Have kids create cross designs. Set the chalk by spraying aerosol hairspray to prevent smearing, then turn the creations into a paper wall quilt.

THE WORD OF OUR GOD

Bible Verse: "The grass withers, the flower fades; but the word of our God will stand forever." (Isaiah 40:8)

Activity: Kids will cherish these amazing laminated bookmarks.

Materials: Bible, paper towels, aluminum foil, one quart plastic freezer bags, permanent marker, dishtowel, iron, watch with a second hand, scissors, grass, small fresh flowers, a cut flower

Ready:

To insure the success of this project, because of the thickness of the plastic, you must use a freezer bag, not a sandwich, storage, or snack bag.

You may want to gather and dry the grass and flowers before meeting with the kids. You'll need a handful of grass and small flowers such as jasmine, honeysuckle, periwinkle, fruit blossoms, herbs, or wildflowers. (Thicker flowers may not press well with this method.) Plan to have at least one flower per child.

To press fresh grass and flowers, turn on the iron to its "hot" setting. Place the blades of grass on one-half of a paper towel. Fold the other half of the towel over the grass, then press the iron directly on the towel for thirty seconds (use the second hand of the watch). Use this same method to press the flowers. When the flowers have cooled, gently loosen them from the towel but leave them on the towel for easier transport.

You may want to make a sample bookmark by following the directions in "Go!"

Set:

Pull out and tear off eight inches or so of the foil, one per child, and place the sheets around the table. On top of each sheet, lay one freezer bag. Put the towels containing the pressed flowers and grass on the table.

Establish your ironing station in a safe area out of the path of the kids. Always use caution when operating an iron around children and do not allow children to use the iron. Spread out the dishtowel as a pad, set out the iron, and have the watch handy.

As kids arrive, let them take turns holding, smelling, and touching the flower.

Go!:

Invite the kids to be seated. Hold up the flower and **ask:** How does this flower smell? Feel? What color is it? After the kids respond, **ask:** What will happen to this flower after one week? *(It will droop; it will begin to lose its flowers; it will die.)*

81

Say: We enjoy colorful flowers and soft grass, but we know that they do not last very long, sometimes one week or sometimes six months, but not forever. The Bible tells us that the things of this world, such as flowers and grass, will not last long. But God's word will last forever.

Open the Bible and read the verse, then have kids say it with you.

Say: God's world comes to us through the Bible. The writings of the Bible are very, very old. Thousands and thousands of seasons of grass and flowers have come and gone, but God's word still stands. To help you remember this verse, we're going to make bookmarks for your Bibles.

Instruct the kids to open their freezer bags, put in a bit of grass, then shake the grass to the bottom of the bag. Next, tell them to select a flower and gently slide it into the bag touching the grass.

As kids do this, plug in the iron and turn it on to "hot," warning children to stay clear of the iron. Next, go around and write each child's name on his or her sheet of foil with the marker.

Direct kids to fold their aluminum foil in half and insert the freezer bag into the fold so that the bottom with the grass and flowers is against the fold.

As each child brings the foil packet to you, press the hot iron directly onto the foil for five seconds only. This is important! Carefully set the hot foil aside for a minute or two until it cools. Let kids pull open the foil to see their newly laminated grass and flowers. Have them trim their creation into a bookmark.

Pray:

Ask kids to gaze upon their bookmarks. **Pray:** Dear God, We're glad your word stands forever. Amen.

Another Go:

Using a Bible dictionary or almanac, show kids the flowers and plants of the Holy Land.

The 23rd Psalm

THE LORD IS MY SHEPHERD

Bible Verse: "The Lord is my shepherd, I shall not want." (Psalm 23:1)

Activity: Using clothespins and scraps, kids will create shepherd dolls.

Materials: Bible; a toy sheep, sheep figurine, or picture of a sheep; clothespins; scraps of fabric; pipe cleaners; markers; glue; scissors

Ready:

This section features eight activities based on the 23rd Psalm. The first six are designed to teach kids each of the six verses of the psalm. The last two activities incorporate the entire psalm. While the activities can stand alone, kids will learn the psalm best if you do the activities in progression. You may want to have kids practice saying the entire psalm at some point during each activity. Also, a word to parents will clue them in that their kids are studying the psalm. Parents may want to reinforce the learning of the psalm by making it a part of family graces or bedtime prayers.

Christian bookstores or catalogs often sell bookmarks, posters, or other items that feature the 23rd Psalm. Consider too, creating your own decorations, such as a poster, mural, or border with the psalm written on it. While the kids are studying the psalm, your pastor and music director may want to include it in the worship service. The psalm may be used in prayers and readings and there are many lovely hymns and anthems with the psalm as lyrics.

The first activity begins by introducing kids to a toy sheep or figurine, who will make a fun mascot throughout all of the activities. If you can't find a toy or figurine, locate a photo or illustration of a sheep, or draw one yourself.

Kids will make shepherd dolls out of clothespins. Precut the fabric into strips and squares, and the pipe cleaners into four-inch lengths, two per doll.

Set:

As kids arrive, point out the sheep and **say:** Go and say hello to our sheep, who needs a name.

Go!

When all the kids have arrived, begin by asking for suggestions for a name for the sheep. When a name has been selected, **say:** We have (*name*) with us today because we're going to be talking about sheep and shepherds. Most shepherds were men but girls and women sometimes cared for sheep too in Bible times, as they have throughout history. A female shepherd is called a "shepherdess."

Next, give kids a bit of background to the book of Psalms. **Say:** The Book of Psalms is a collection of poems. Many of these poems were sung in the temple as part of the Hebrew worship service. Of all the psalms, the most famous is Psalm 23.

Open the Bible and read Psalm 23, then ask the kids to say verse one along with you.

Continue: Scholars believe that David wrote many of the psalms, including this one. David, who became the King of Israel, worked as a shepherd when he was a young man. David understood how it felt to be a shepherd and care for a flock of sheep. He knew that a good shepherd made certain his sheep had green grass for grazing and fresh water for drinking. He protected them from wild animals and searched for any sheep that were lost. In Psalm 23, David compares God to a shepherd.

Say the first verse again. Then **ask:** How is God like a shepherd to us? *(He guides us; he loves us; he listens to our prayers and helps us when we are troubled.)*

Tell the kids that as a reminder that God is our shepherd, they will now make their own shepherd dolls to keep. Give each child a clothespin and set out the glue, scissors, fabric strips and squares, pipe cleaners, and markers. Demonstrate how to make the shepherd doll: Wrap a length of pipe cleaner beneath the head of the clothespin for arms. Glue a square of fabric around the body for the robe and a strip of fabric over the head for a headpiece. Using a marker, add eyes and a mouth. Finally, bend another length of pipe cleaner to be a staff and twist one of the doll's arms around it.

Pray:

When the kids have finished their shepherds, have them hold them in their hands. Ask them to bow their heads and close their eyes as you **pray:** Dear God, The Lord is my shepherd, I shall not want. Thank you for loving and caring for us as a shepherd cares for sheep. Amen.

Another Go:

Consider recruiting two teenagers or adults to dress as shepherds and present a dialogue titled the "The Shepherd's Conversation" found in *Flood Punch, Bowl Bread and Group Soup: 60 Multi-age Activities for Christian Kids* (Lisa Flinn and Barbara Younger, Abingdon Press, 2001.)

In Green Pastures

Bible Verse: "He makes me lie down in green pastures; he leads me beside still waters; he restores my soul." (Psalm 23:2)

Activity: Kids will celebrate the significance of the color green at a Green Pastures Party.

Materials: Bible, a green marker or crayon, a green tablecloth, green cups, plates, and napkins, snacks and a drink

Ready:

You will need the green tablecloth to create the green pasture. Green tableware is not necessary but will add to the atmosphere. Consider other green decorations such as garlands, crepe paper streamers, or balloons. If possible, since you are leading the kids to green pastures, plan on taking them to another space in the church to discover the pasture. In warmer weather, you may want to hold this activity outdoors.

For the snack, you may serve foods that are naturally green such as broccoli with dip, guacamole with chips, lime gelatin, grapes, or green apples but kids will have fun with foods that you color green with food coloring, too. Consider adding coloring to pudding, cookies, cupcakes, lemonade and/or vanilla yogurt. Pack the snack in a basket or other portable container.

Set:

Before kids arrive, spread out the green tablecloth in the place where you will be holding the Green Pastures Party.

Go!

After you call the kids together, begin by holding up the green marker or crayon. **Say:** The second verse of the 23rd Psalm celebrates this color. When I count to three, I want you to all call out what this color is.

Next, open the Bible and read the verse, then have the kids say it with you.

Ask: Why was it important for a shepherd to find green pastures? *(The flock needed fresh, green grass for grazing.)* **Say:** This verse helps us understand that God will take us to green places. Green places are the things that we need in life such as food and shelter. The verse also talks about still waters. Rushing water can be dangerous. Still water represents places that are safe and secure.

Tell the kids that now they are going to look for a green pasture. Lead them to the green tablecloth, taking a roundabout route if practical to add to the fun. When you are almost there, **say:** Look! A green pasture where we can rest. And I'm so glad there is still water nearby.

85

When you arrive at the green pasture, ask kids to say the verse again, then invite them to lie down and relax. After a minute or two, **ask:** The verse says that being led to green pastures and still waters restores the soul. What does this mean? *(That these places help us to rest and also to feel the presence of God.)*

Have the kids rest for another minute or two, then announce that after a prayer, they are invited to a Green Pastures Party.

Pray:

Ask the kids to close their eyes while they continue to lie down. **Pray:** Dear God, Thank you for the Green Pastures Party that we are about to enjoy, and thank you for the green places in our lives. We're glad that you make us lie down in green pastures, and that you lead us beside still waters, and that you restore our souls. Amen.

Serve the green refreshments.

Another Go:

Cut small sprigs of evergreen, soaking them for a few hours to enable the sprigs to stay fresh. Before you give each child a bit of evergreen, explain that evergreen is a symbol of God's never-ending love, a love that is ever fresh and ever green.

IN RIGHT PATHS

Bible Verse: " He leads me in right paths for his name's sake."
(Psalm 23:3)

Activity: Kids will follow signs to help them make certain that they are on the right path.

Materials: Bible, paper, markers or crayons, tape, small prizes, or snack

Ready:

For the game, you will need to write "Right Path" on separate sheets of paper to be taped to doors, walls, and walkways. You will also need one sign that says: "Congratulations! You have taken the right path and are in the right spot to end the game."

Walk out a route, then decide where you will tape the signs and how many you will need. The signs will lead kids around the church. Plan on leaving small prizes such as stickers or bookmarks, or a snack, at the ending spot.

Set:

Tape the "Right Path" signs to places along the route and the "Congratulations" sign at the ending spot. The small prizes or snack should be placed at the ending spot, too.

As kids come into the room, **say:** You've taken the right path to come and join us today. I'm so glad that you are here!

Go!

Call the kids together to begin. **Ask:** Do you ever have trouble making decisions? After the kids respond, share a decision or two that you have found difficult. Then **ask:** Have you ever felt that God has helped you make a decision? After the kids respond, once again you may want to share one of your own experiences. **Say:** God can help us make decisions. Prayer, listening to the advice of other Christians and listening to our own hearts, and reading the Bible can all be helpful in decision-making.

Open the Bible and read the verse, then have the kids say it with you.

Say: The right paths that God leads us in are the right decisions that we make. "For his name's sake" means that we try to make the right decisions to honor God.

Explain that kids will now play the Right Paths Game. They are to figure out the right way to go until they reach the ending spot. Don't tell them ahead of time that there are signs to guide them, just send them on their way.

Pray:

Once kids have followed the right path, ask them to join hands or link elbows for a prayer. **Pray:** Dear God, Help us to make good decisions. Thank you for leading us in the right path. We pray for your name's sake. Amen.

Another Go:

Ask kids to choose partners and take turns leading one another on the right paths. (Do this in a safe location where there aren't stairs or other hazards.) One partner must keep eyes tightly shut while the other leads.

For You Are With Me

Bible Verse: "Even though I walk through the darkest valley, I fear no evil; for you are with me; your rod and your staff—they comfort me." (Psalm 23:4)

Activity: After learning about the shepherd's tools of rod and staff, kids will create edible staffs.

Materials: Bible, canned breadstick dough, baking sheets, timer, potholders, spatula, napkins

Ready:

You will need access to an oven for this activity. Kids will twist and shape breadstick dough into shepherd staffs. One can of dough usually makes twelve breadsticks. You may want to count on two breadsticks per child.

Set:

Preheat the oven to the temperature suggested on the can of breadstick dough.

As kids arrive, put your arm around each of them and **say:** I'm so glad that you are going to be in our flock today.

Go!

Gather the kids together and **ask:** When you came in this morning, I put my arm around you. How does it feel when someone puts an arm around you? After the kids respond, **say:** When someone puts an arm around us, we feel loved and secure. There is a verse in the 23rd Psalm that expresses this thought. In this verse, the rod and staff are symbols of God's love and comfort. Even in the scariest and saddest times of our life, God is with us.

Open the Bible and read the verse, then have the kids say it with you.

Explain that a shepherd used the rod to protect the sheep from wolves and other dangerous animals. Rods were also used to help count the sheep to see if any were missing. The staff, with a crook on one end, was used to gather the sheep together and to help rescue a lost sheep from a crevice or water.

Next tell the kids that they are going to make edible shepherd's staffs. Show them how to twist and then shape the dough into a staff. Make certain both ends of the staffs are pressed onto the baking sheet so they do not come unraveled while baking. Once the staffs are in the oven, set the timer according to the directions on the package. Breadsticks burn easily, so make certain to check on them promptly.

Pray:

While the shepherd's staffs are baking, tell kids that they are gong to pretend that each of their arms is a shepherd's staff. Have them stand in a circle with one arm crooked around the person to their right and another arm crooked around the person to their left. **Pray:** Dear God, The next time we are sad or lonely or worried, we will remember this verse: "Even though I walk through the darkest valley, I fear no evil, for you are with me; your rod and your staff—they comfort me." (Psalm 23:4) Amen.

When the shepherd staffs are finished, allow them to cool for a minute or two before removing them with the spatula and serving them on napkins.

Another Go:

Have your kids make sympathy cards for someone in your congregation who has lost a loved one. Kids may want to draw shepherds and/or sheep and write all or part of the verse on the card.

ANOINT MY HEAD WITH OIL

Bible Verse: "You prepare a table before me in the presence of my enemies; you anoint my head with oil; my cup overflows." (Psalm 23:5)

Activity: After filling cups of cereal to overflowing, kids will take turns anointing one another with oil.

Materials: Bible, cereal, cups, large bowl, olive oil, small bowls, tissues

Ready:

For the opening activity, you will need a cereal that kids especially like. As they arrive, they will fill a cup until it overflows with the cereal.

After they learn the verse, kids will anoint one another with oil. Although olive oil was used in Bible days, you may substitute another type of cooking oil if need be.

Set:

Pour the cereal into a large bowl and have the cups nearby. As kids arrive, invite them to fill a cup until it overflows.

Go!:

When everyone has had a chance to fill a cup, invite the kids to be seated and snack on the cereal. **Ask:** How did it feel to fill your cup until it overflowed? After the kids respond, **say:** When you were invited to fill a cup until it overflowed, you knew you were going to get a generous helping. There is a verse in the 23rd Psalm that talks about a cup that overflows.

Open the Bible and read the verse, then have the kids say it with you.

Continue: This verse in the 23rd Psalm talks about the good things that God brings into our lives: a table of food prepared for us and a cup that is so full it overflows.

Say the verse again. **Ask:** Does anyone know what the part of the verse that says "You anoint my head with oil" means? After the kids respond, **say:** In Bible times, people were sometimes anointed with oil when they became leaders, when they were sick, or as a sign of welcome and friendship. This part of the verse speaks of God bestowing this loving gesture on us.

Explain that as a symbol of God's love for us, the kids will now take turns anointing one another's foreheads with oil. Pour small amounts of oil into the bowl or bowls. Assign partners. Kids are to dip a thumb into the oil and place it on their partner's forehead, **saying**: I anoint your head with oil. Have tissues available for wiping off the oil.

Pray:

When the anointing is finished, ask kids to bow their heads and close their eyes. **Pray:** Dear God: "You prepare a table before me in the presence of my enemies; you anoint my head with oil; my cup overflows." (Psalm 23:5) Truly you have blessed us! Amen.

Another Go!:

Kids will have fun decorating plastic cups with permanent markers. They can take the cups home and remember God's good gifts to them as they fill their cups almost to overflowing!

Surely Goodness and Mercy

Bible Verse: "Surely goodness and mercy shall follow me all the days of my life, and I shall dwell in the house of the Lord my whole life long." (Psalm 23:6)

Activity: Kids will decorate Goodness and Mercy Journals in which to record their thoughts and observations

Materials: Bible, posterboard or large sheet of paper, marker, note books, glue, paint pens or markers, birthday stickers, wrapping paper, party invitations, and ribbon, new pens or pencils

Ready:

Purchase notebooks with either a plain or a marble cover for kids to decorate. Although larger notebooks are best for both decorating and writing, medium-sized or smaller will do. Kids will first use the paint pens or markers to write their birthdays on the cover of the notebooks. Then they will decorate the covers with birthday stickers, scraps of wrapping paper, a party invitation, and/or bits of ribbon. Make a sample journal to show them. Plan on giving each child a newly sharpened pencil or pen.

Set:

Print today's date at the top of the posterboard. As the kids arrive, ask them to write down something for which they are thankful.

Go!

When all have arrived, **say:** Today, (say the date), one of the days of your life, you wrote down something for which you were thankful. Read the list. Then **say:** The last verse of the 23rd Psalm talks about the good things that God brings into the days of our lives.

Open the Bible and read the verse, then have the kids say it with you.

Continue: This verse talks about the goodness and mercy of God in our lives. "Goodness" means not only the good things in our lives, but the good things that we do, and other people do, to help one another. "Mercy" means kindness or compassion. God is merciful to us because God loves us and forgives our sins. We can show mercy to others by forgiving them when they hurt us.

Next, ask kids to come up with examples of goodness that have been bestowed on them and goodness they have bestowed on others. Then ask kids to come up with examples of mercy.

Say: Every day, throughout all the days of your lives, if you pay attention, you will find examples of goodness and mercy. To help you carefully watch for and then remember this goodness and mercy, we're going to make Goodness and Mercy Journals. We'll decorate them with a birthday theme, since your birthday was the very first day of all the days of your life.

Give out the notebooks and put out paint pens or markers, the birthday items, glue, and scissors. Show kids the sample, then set them to work. You may need to assist younger kids in writing their birthdays on the cover.

When the journals are finished, give each child a brand new pencil or pen.

Pray:

Ask kids to record one example of goodness and mercy in their journals that they have seen yesterday or today. (Kids who do not write yet may draw pictures.)

Then ask them to put down their journals and pencils while you **pray:** Dear God, We plan to use these Goodness and Mercy journals to record the goodness and mercy in our lives. As the psalm says: "Surely goodness and mercy shall follow me all the days of my life, and I shall dwell in the house of the Lord my whole life long." (Psalm 23:6) Amen.

Another Go:

Play the Alphabet Blessings Game. Everyone sits in a circle. The first person names a blessing that starts with A; the next person names that blessing and one that starts with B; the next person says the A and B blessing and adds a C blessing. This continues until the alphabet is finished.

A SHEPHERD'S ADVENTURE

Bible Verse: The 23rd Psalm

Activity: Kids will travel back to Bible days to experience the life of a shepherd.

Materials: Bible (or copy of the 23rd Psalm), paper, marker, tape or pushpins, yarn, snack, baskets, plates, cups, and napkins, a shepherd's costume

Ready:

During this activity, kids will stop at six Adventure Stops. You will mark each spot with a sign that says "Adventure Stop # 1," "Adventure Stop #2," and so on. Make a sign for each stop.

You will play the role of the shepherd who leads the kids in the adventure. A shepherd's costume is easily created with bathrobes, sheets, and/or assorted fabric that can be draped and pinned. Study the script ahead of time so that you can more naturally play the role of the shepherd.

For the snack, plan on serving food that a shepherd might have consumed in Bible times such as dried fruits, cheese, and flatbread or pita bread. Pack the snack and plates, cups, and napkins into a basket. For drinks, you may serve water or grape juice.

This activity works best outdoors but if this isn't practical, it can take place in a fellowship hall or in various locations in the church. Wherever you will be holding the adventure, decide where each Adventure Stop will be.

Set:

Place the Adventure Stop signs at each stop. The first sign should be on the door to your room. Create the yarn path at Adventure Stop # 3 leading to Adventure Stop #4 and leave the snack at Adventure Stop #5.

Don your shepherd's costume. As kids enter the room greet them, and **say:** Welcome. I am your shepherd guide, and today I am taking you on a Shepherd's Adventure.

Go!:

When the kids have all arrived, gather them together and begin. **Say:** I am a shepherd/shepherdess from Bible days. Before I take you on the adventure, I'd like to say with you the 23rd Psalm, a psalm that speaks of the life of a shepherd.

Lead the kids in saying the psalm.

Next say: We will visit six Adventure Stops; and at each stop, we will think about one of the six verses of the psalm. This is our first stop, Adventure Stop #1. Here you met me, your shepherd guide. Let's say the first verse of the psalm.

Have the kids say verse one with you, then lead them to the next stop.

Say: Here's Adventure Stop #2: Lovely green pastures. Lead kids in saying verse two. Invite them to rest and visit with one another for a few minutes before moving on to the next stop.

Say: Here's Adventure Stop #3. It looks like we have a path ahead. Have kids say verse three with you, then lead them on the yarn path to the next stop. As you go, make plenty of comments such as: "I hope we've decided to take the right path" and "I like to remember that God is leading me." Move on to the next stop.

Say: Here's Adventure Stop #4. Oh my goodness! I see a wolf in the distance. But I have my pretend rod to chase him off. (Pretend to chase off a wolf.) Pause a minute and then **say:** Time to count the flock. Count for a bit, then **say:** Oh my! I'm one short! A lamb is missing! (Lead the kids a few yards away from the stop.) Look down and **say:** She's caught on that rocky ledge. I'll use my pretend staff to pull her to safety. (Pull the lamb to safety.) Then **say:** A shepherd's job can be scary, but I know that God is with me and comforts me. Lead the kids in saying verse four before moving on to the next stop.

Say: Here's Adventure Stop #5. Gosh I'm getting hungry. Look! A basket. Peek into the basket, then **continue:** Food and drink! God has prepared a table for us and filled our cups to overflowing. Lead the kids in saying verse five, then serve the snack. When the snack is finished, have the kids help you clean up, then move on to the last stop.

Once you have reached the church steps, **say:** Here we are at our final Adventure stop, Adventure Stop #6. What a wonderful adventure we've had. God has blessed our lives in so many ways. Lead kids in saying the final verse, then the entire psalm.

Pray:

Ask kids to close their eyes and bow their heads. **Pray:** Dear God, We thank you for all of the goodness and mercy you have brought into our lives. Thank you for this Shepherd's Adventure, thank you for one another, and thank you for your house, our church. Amen.

Conclude by saying: I'm so glad you could come along on this adventure today. May God bless each and every one of you!

Another Go:

Candy canes were created by a candy maker in honor of the Christmas shepherds and the staffs they carried. Give kids a candy cane (many flavors are available year round) as an edible souvenir of the Shepherd's Adventure.

SHARING THE PSALM

Bible Verse: The 23rd Psalm

Activity: After creating sheep puppets, kids will present the psalm to other groups in the church.

Materials: Bible, small paper bags, cotton balls, glue, crayons or markers

Ready:

Plan on having your kids use their puppets to present the 23rd Psalm to other groups at church. This activity works well during the Sunday school hour, but there may be other occasions too such as Bible school, a worship service, or a fellowship event. If a field trip is a possibility, consider having your kids bring their puppets along to a nursing home or to visit shut-ins or the elderly in your congregation.

Make a sample puppet. With a dark crayon or marker, draw the face of a sheep onto the folded bottom flap of a paper bag. Make certain the face is above the body of the bag. Then glue cotton balls onto the main part of the bag to create the sheep's fleece.

Set:

Make any final arrangements for the presentation of the psalm.

As kids arrive, put your hand into your puppet and move the head up and down with your fingertips as you have the sheep **say:** Today we're going to say the whole psalm. Baa…

Go!:

Have your puppet say: "Come on everybody, we're ready to start." When the kids are seated, say to your puppet: "Thanks for helping me greet everyone. Now I want you to rest for a bit while we practice the psalm and then make a flock of friends for you."

Continue: We've been studying the 23rd Psalm. **Ask:** Can someone show me where the psalm is located in the Bible? After a child finds the psalm, ask for a volunteer to read it.

Spend a few minutes reviewing the verses and any and all activities that you've shared together to reinforce those verses. Then **say:** Although we can always read the psalm from our Bibles, knowing the psalm by memory is helpful, too. There are times in your life when you may not have a Bible with you. If you know the 23rd by heart, then you can say it anytime.

Next, lead the kids in practicing the psalm two or three times.

Pick up the puppet and have it say: "Hey, wait a minute! You promised to make me a flock of friends." Look at the puppet and say: "Oh, you're right! I did promise a flock of friends for you."

Bring out the craft supplies and have the kids each make a sheep puppet.

Pray:

While the glue is drying on the puppets, **say:** Many Christians say the 23rd Psalm as a prayer. Now that you know the psalm by heart, you may want to use it in your prayers, too. Ask kids to bow their heads and close their eyes and join you in saying the psalm. **Pray:** Dear God, Hear us as we say together the 23rd Psalm. Amen.

Next have your sheep puppet greet the new flock of friends. Let kids practice making their puppets say the psalm before presenting the psalm to other groups now or at the planned time.

Another Go:

Let kids use their puppets to practice two other beloved verses in the Bible that speak of sheep and shepherds: Psalm 100: 3b: "We are his people, and the sheep of his pasture" and John 10:11: "I am the good shepherd. The good shepherd lays down his life for the sheep."